Your First
O GAUGE LAYOUT

Featuring MTH trains and accessories

Mike Ashey

KALMBACH
BOOKS

Printed in the United States of America

00 01 02 03 04 05 06 07 08   10 9 8 7 6 5 4 3 2 1

Visit our website at http://kalmbachbooks.com
Secure online ordering available

Publisher's Cataloging-in-Publication
(Provided by Quality Books, Inc.)

Ashey, Mike. 200
    Your first O gauge layout / Mike Ashey. —
1st ed.
    p. cm.
    ISBN: 0-89778-465-0

    1. Railroads—Models. I. Title.

TF197.A84 2000   625.1'9
                    QBI00-500168

Book and cover design: Kristi Ludwig

MTH Trademarks: M.T.H. Electric Trains®, Premier Line®, Proto-Sound®, RailKing®, Real Trax®, Z-750™, Z-4000™. Lionel® is a registered trademark of Lionel L.L.C., Chesterfield, Michigan.

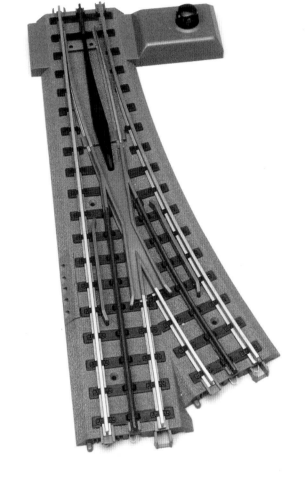

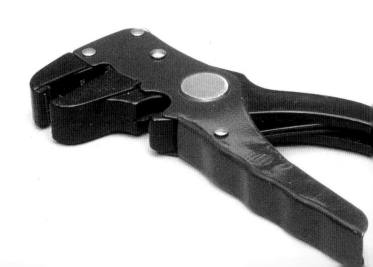

Contents

Dedication

To my sons, Thomas and Gregory

Acknowledgements

Many thanks to Mike Wolf, Andy Edleman, and Joe Rauseo of M.T.H. Electric Trains for supplying me with great trains, accessories, track plans, and technical advice; to Dean Johnson of PDK Trains, Ocala, Florida, and Kirk Mitchell of Just Trains, Newark, Delaware, for allowing me to pick their knowledgeable brains on O gauge railroading; to Terry Spohn, formerly of Kalmbach Publishing Co., for his support; to my wife, Kelly, for her patience and her editing skills; and finally to my sons, Thomas and Gregory, for giving me the time I needed to complete this book and for their help on the layout.

Foreword

Like so many other adults who remember their childhood experiences with Lionel and American Flyer electric trains, I wanted to re-create those great memories for my two sons. I also wanted to rekindle the excitement within myself that I once felt as a child—there is something special about building an O gauge layout and watching a steam locomotive chug down the track puffing smoke.

As I started looking into the world of O gauge electric trains after being away for many years, the first thing I noticed was that much has changed: there are new manufacturers, new ideas, and new products. Information on the latest developments was available here and there, yet I was unable to locate a single reference that could explain the basics. I was lacking a resource that could remove the gray cloud of confusion and get me going on setting up a decent layout, complete with scenery, with minimal effort.

Having written several scale modeling books, I found it a natural leap to write a beginner's book for O gauge railroaders and parents who want to introduce their children to the exciting world of O gauge electric trains. I have packed as much information as I could into this book; much of it is in the pictures themselves. They say a picture is worth a thousand words, and I think you'll agree that looking at a picture greatly enhances a written explanation. With pictures you readily see how to use basic carpentry skills to build a sturdy train board, use good wiring techniques for the minimal amount of wiring you will have to do for track and accessories, or build a hill or mountain.

As I started learning more about the manufacturers of O gauge trains, I was impressed with the products of relative newcomer M.T.H. Electric Trains. They have truly taken O gauge railroading into the 21st century by designing their trains for "plug-and-play" use. All their products are designed to draw power directly from the track. What this means is that all you have to do is snap their track together, plug in accessory sensors and accessories, turn on the transformer, and away you go. With MTH's new track design you can even run the trains on carpet. In a minimal amount of time you and your children will be running trains and getting inspiration for expanding your layout.

I have distilled all the knowledge, skills, and techniques necessary to understand O gauge railroading, build a train board, lay out track and wire it along with accessories, and add scenery. All these things are conveyed through brief introductory text followed by step-by-step pictures and captions.

Letting your children participate in creating a layout teaches them organizational skills, planning and implementation techniques, basic carpentry and electrical wiring, and analytical thinking through problem solving. It will also fire their imaginations and expand the boundaries of their creativity. But best of all, it will be fun today and tomorrow.

I think I have accomplished what I set out to achieve. Have fun O gauge railroading, spend quality time with your children, and most of all, keep it all in perspective!

Mike Ashey

Chapter One
The Basics

Welcome to the hobby of model railroading—toy train style. Perhaps you're old enough to remember the O gauge trains of the 1940s and '50s. You can still find them. In fact, Lionel trains and track are still in production, and the new trains are compatible with the old trains of the '50s. Oh, the new ones look and run better, but at heart they're still the trains you loved as a child.

Lionel trains—old and new—are available at many hobby shops and train shows held all over the country throughout the year. And there are other manufacturers making Lionel-compatible trains from which to choose.

While you can build the layout in this book (more or less) using Lionel or other equipment, I chose to use the products of M.T.H. Electric Trains. The world of MTH 21st Century "plug-and-play" railroading is an exciting one.

et's start off with describing what I mean by plug-and-play railroading. MTH Electric trains have taken a whole new approach to model railroading by applying the concepts developed in the world of home computers. That is to say, all it takes to get a computer and its accessories going is to plug it in.

MTH has applied this same concept to O and O27 gauge trains. No longer is it necessary to cut track sections to make a layout fit together, insulate track sections, or understand the basics of electricity to wire a switch or an accessory. You won't have to worry about your children cutting their hands on the edges of the track sections as they try to put them together. Nor will you have to fool with laying roadbed, adding track, and then spending hours adding gravel around the track and over the roadbed to simulate real track.

MTH's new track system even works well on a floor or carpet. With MTH track and accessories you just snap the track sections together, snap in the switches and accessory activation devices, plug in the accessories and the transformer, add a locomotive and some rolling stock, and away you go! It's as simple as that.

Before we delve into the specifics, let's address one key issue. Why large scale trains (as compared to the more popular, but smaller, HO or N scale)? If the trains are for your child (as well as yourself, of course) then O gauge is the way to go. The large

size of the trains makes them easy for children to handle, especially when placing the trains on the track, fixing derailments, and coupling and uncoupling rolling stock. MTH's plug-and-play concept makes it especially quick and easy for parents or children to set up the trains and accessories without major wiring. In fact, all the accessories, including the track switches, draw their power right from the track.

Larger scale means the trains can be built stronger, which is a real plus with children. For some reason children just love to make the trains go fast, which means that the locomotives and rolling stock will jump the tracks on many occasions.

Another thing children do often is crash trains, and so the stronger the trains are made, the better they will hold up to abuse. Having strong metal die-cast or ABS-plastic bodies, metal undercarriages, and metal trucks and couplers means that the trains are hefty and are built tough and rugged. In short, O or larger is the way to go where kids are involved.

What are gauge and scale?

With newcomers there is always confusion with respect to gauge and scale, and the differences between O and O27 electric trains. First, let's deal with the terms "gauge" and "scale." Gauge is simply the distance between the rails. As an example, on a real railroad the distance between the rails (gauge) is 4 feet, 8½ inches. The distance

between the two outside rails on O gauge track is 1¼ inches.

The term "scale" simply refers to the size relationship between the real thing and a model. In O scale, the model is 1/48 the size of the real thing. (A caveat: These are called "toy" trains, suggesting that they probably will not be perfectly exact-scale models, though many are nearly so.)

Now let's talk about the differences between O and O27. As I mentioned, Lionel and MTH O gauge trains are (roughly) 1/48 scale models. Since a 1/48 scale locomotive and 1/48 scale piece of rolling stock are fairly long, they require wide-diameter curves to negotiate without jumping the track. Certain long locomotives and some large pieces of rolling stock, like passenger cars, need large-diameter curves of 42 inches, 54 inches, even 72 inches. These translate into a pretty big layout, even if you're just setting up an oval.

The housing boom and the baby boom that occurred after World War II created two big challenges for the Lionel Corporation, at that time the leading manufacturer of electric trains. How could they market their trains to the millions of new families that were having children, and how could they redesign their trains to fit into the millions of smaller homes being built? While the marketing end of the challenge is all Lionel history, the technical aspects of the challenge is where we need to focus our discussion.

To solve the space problem the Lionel Corporation created the O27 line of trains. They redesigned their standard O gauge track so that the height of the rails was ⅛ inch lower while keeping the distance between the rails (gauge) the same. They also designed a 27-inch curve, which is a pretty small curve, but one which would easily fit in a small room. Hence the term O27 was adopted. The "O" means that it's O gauge and

the "27" means that it's a 27-inch-diameter curve, or that it's a locomotive or piece of rolling stock designed to run on a 27-inch curve. To get 1/48 scale trains to make a 27-inch curve, Lionel had to reduce the height, length, and width—hence the scale—of its rolling stock and locomotives to negotiate the tighter curves. What this translated into was that the locomotives and rolling stock were smaller than 1/48 scale. In actuality, Lionel produced many different types of O27 locomotives and cars with slightly different scales, all smaller than 1/48 scale, and also slightly different in scale from each other.

Those are the fundamentals of the matter. But to confuse the issue, one year an O gauge locomotive would appear in an "O gauge" set and the next year in an "O27 set," depending on the marketing needs and strategies of Lionel at the time. Many—though not all—pieces can run on both O and O27 track.

Today the scale/gauge issue continues in fact, if not in name. For example, MTH's Premier line is their O gauge, 1/48 scale trains; their RailKing line, the equivalent of Lionel's old O27 trains, is made up of cars and locomotives slightly smaller than 1/48 scale. Keep in mind that if you decide to purchase O27 gauge track, that does not mean that you are limited to just 27-inch diameter curves. Several different diameters are available: 31-inch, 42-inch, 54-inch and 72-inch curves.

I recommend that you visit your local train hobby store to become familiar with the different manufacturers, their product lines, and the available accessories. While you are there, pick up a model railroad magazine that focuses on O gauge railroading. The best two are *Classic Toy Trains* and *O Gauge Model Railroading*. These magazines have numerous articles and advertisements from manufacturers, hobby stores and mail order businesses. In addition, you will acquire their website addresses, which also contain a lot of information.

Track, transformers, and accessories

From the earliest days of electric trains, more than a hundred years ago, the standard track construction for O gauge trains has been thin-metal tube construction for the rails and thin-metal boxes for the ties, three or four per track section. The individual track lengths are attached to each other with metal pin connectors, and the tracks have to be pushed together, which can on occasion lead to cut hands.

Although the tracks are strong, the connector pins loosen and pull out, electrical contact between the track sections is affected, the metal rusts over time, and the tracks look rather unrealistic. In addition, the trains make a lot of noise rolling across the tracks.

To improve the appearance of the track and reduce the noise level model railroaders sometimes place cork roadbed or other sound-deadening materials under the track. To improve the appearance of the track, additional ties can be added using strips of balsa or rubber, and scale gravel is then added around the track and the cork roadbed. All of this translates into a lot of work.

Over the years manufacturers have produced track that has rails made from solid metal. This makes them look more realistic, reduces the chance of cuts, and provides for better electrical contact. While these new track designs solved some of the problems that plagued O gauge track for almost 100 years, the problems of noise, appearance, and special wiring needs still existed. When accessories were added that were activated by a passing train, special care had to be taken to either make or purchase insulated track sections and then add wiring to power the accessory and activate it.

The addition of track switches also required special wiring. While the switches could be powered directly from the tracks, the power draw from the switch motor was so high that it affected the operation of the trains, resulting in the need for an alternate power supply and special wiring.

M.T.H. Electric Trains has solved these problems by integrating roadbed into the track design (called "Real Trax") and using solid metal for the rails. The roadbed is made from thick, high-impact plastic. The individual track sections snap together, and each section has positive electrical clips built into the underside of the track. This innovative track design allows the track to be set up on just about any surface, including rugs, which makes setting up a train set under the Christmas tree a breeze.

MTH also designed an entire array of accessories that draw their power from the track. In addition, the accessories are activated by simply plugging an infrared sensor into the track and connecting the sensor to the accessory. When a train passes the sensor, the infrared switch activates the accessory. After the train passes, the sensor turns off, thereby turning off the accessory. MTH even built in adjustable delay times for the sensor switch and also a distance sensitivity adjustment for the infrared beam.

Track switches are simply snapped into place; three wires run from the turnout directly to the toggle, which throws the turnout. Here again, the switches draw their power directly from the track. One would think that all this power being drawn from the track would impact the operation of the trains. MTH has designed its switches and accessories to draw so little voltage that there is no effect on the operation of the trains at all. Accessories, switches, and infrared sensors can be powered from an optional power supply. The term "plug-and-play" is truly appropriate.

To minimize the issue of having to cut lengths of track to complete a layout, MTH offers several different short track lengths for both straight and curved track. The straight track lengths are 3½, 4¼, 5, and 5½ inches long, and half-length curved track is available in 31- and 42-inch diameters. The standard straight track length is 10 inches, but 30-inch lengths are also available.

Curved tracks make 31-, 42- and 72-inch diameter circles, and while the 72-inch curve is for a large layout, both the 31-inch and the 42-inch curves will fit a variety of configurations for 4 x 8-foot layouts.

Crossover and uncoupling tracks are available, as are adapter tracks, which will allow you to connect your Real Trax to traditional O gauge track. Switches come as left- and right-hand, with diverging routes for 31-, 42- and 72-inch curves. The turnout motors simply unplug and snap in, and you can easily flip the motors from one side of the switch to the other. The switches also have a

non-derailing feature so that if a train approaches a switch that is set in the wrong direction, the switch will automatically throw to the correct direction so that the locomotive will not derail.

MTH has also incorporated the plug-and-play concept in their transformer designs. Simply plugging in the electrical leads from the transformer to the track "lock-on" sends power to the track, sensors, and accessories. The standard transformer that comes with each MTH set, the Z-750, provides 75 watts of power—more than enough power to run any locomotive on a 4 x 8-foot layout including switches and track-activated and powered accessories. The Z-750 has bell, horn, and direction buttons, and it can be used to control any manufacturer's locomotive-equipped sound system.

Another nice feature of MTH transformers is that they can also power vintage Lionel locomotives; not all modern transformers can do this.

MTH also designed their large transformer—the Z-4000—to accommodate accessories that do not run off track power, like street and building lights. If you prefer to run all your accessories from a separate power source, the Z-4000 is the way to go. This transformer can run two trains, and it also runs and programs all of the Proto-Sound effects incorporated in MTH or other manufacturers' locomotives (in addition to

the horn, bell, and direction buttons). The programming feature is great, as you can set which sound features you want as well as the level of sound. The Z-4000 also has a built-in cooling fan, which is great to have because children, and sometimes adults, forget to turn off the transformer. The fan will keep the transformer cool, and this translates into an extended life. The Z-4000 also has an overload indicator and pop-out fuses just in case.

MTH has many different types of operating accessories that can be activated with an infrared sensor, including crossing gate signals, banjo signals, and semaphores. These accessories have tiny internal motors that operate the working parts. In addition, MTH also markets accessories such as highway flashing signals, railroad block signals, and signal bridges, to name a few, that change light colors or flash. MTH also has many different kinds of illuminated, die-cast street lights to choose from, which are also well built. They also have telephone pole sets, road signs, and high-tension electrical towers that have the same girder construction framing as the real ones. They even offer operating street traffic signal lights.

MTH has several different types of bridges, including their beautiful steel-arch bridge and their massive Hell Gate bridge. You can buy single- and double-wide tunnel portals if you like to build mountains and run your trains through them. MTH also has several different operating buildings, such as their operating gas station, firehouse, and station platform. The gas station has a car that emerges from the garage as the door opens up, and the firehouse has a beautiful fire engine that rolls out of the open doors. The operating station platform has people that disappear as trains leave the platform. In keeping with the plug-and-play concept, MTH offers their buildings as structures preassembled. You can buy a two-story house, three-story buildings, and even a complete train station. These structures are well built and designed so that you can add interior details and even weather them if you like so that they appear more realistic.

Locomotives and rolling stock

There are three basic types of locomotives: steam, diesel, and electric. Steam locomotives are by far the favorite of most O gauge model railroaders, probably because of all the working siderods and the smoke units. Many variations of wheel and drive combinations are available; their designations are based on a simple principle. All steam locomotives have three numbers associated with them. The first number is the total number of small forward wheels, the second number is the total number of drive wheels, and the third number is the total of small rear wheels. As an example, 4-8-0 would mean that there are 4 forward wheels (on two axles), 8 drive wheels (on four axles), and no rear wheels.

All MTH O gauge steam locomotives are also equipped with a smoke unit, front lights, and a whistle. Diesel and electric locomotives do not have the exterior moving parts steam engines do, but unlike the typical black color of steam locomotives, diesel and electric locomotives are very colorful. In addition, the shapes of diesel and electric locomotives are all different, which adds to their unique appearances.

All MTH diesel and electric locomotives are equipped with horns, front lights, and illuminated cab. Several manufacturers have taken advantage of the breakthroughs in digital sound recordings and have incorporated the real sounds of steam, diesel, and electric locomotives into a digital format. MTH's sound system is called Proto-Sound, and all their locomotives are available with this system for an additional charge.

MTH locomotives also have what is commonly referred to as an E-unit. The E-unit is an internal electrical switch that changes from forward to neutral to reverse when transformer power is turned off and on. What this translates into is that if you are moving a locomotive forward and you then bring it to a stop, the E-unit will switch to the neutral position. If you apply transformer power to the locomotive it will not move, but since power has been applied to the track you can throw track switches. When you once again shut down the transformer power, the E-unit will switch to the reverse mode, so that when you power up again the locomotive will go in reverse. While this sequence (traditional and unique to toy trains) sounds odd, it can really be handy, and children seem to master it quickly.

MTH has a complete line of rolling stock and passenger cars in all shapes, colors, and road names. Their passenger trains range from old early-20th-century-style heavyweights to modern designs in several differ-

ent road names and color schemes. Their rolling stock spans the full range of just about anything that has rolled down the tracks. There are single-, double-, and triple-dome tank cars; hopper cars with and without coal loads; box, stock, and refrigerator cars; flatcars and gondolas with and without loads; crane cars; searchlight cars; and last but not least, cabooses of several different designs and variations. MTH even has snowplow cars. All of MTH's passenger and freight cars are well made and built to last. Their trucks, wheels, and couplers are metal, which is important because they last a lot longer than comparable plastic pieces, they are stronger, and the couplers will not wear out or uncouple when there are too many cars coupled together. Some of their designs even have individual springs on the trucks, which greatly enhance their appearance.

MTH manufactures two separate lines of O gauge trains—Premier and RailKing. The Premier line is true O gauge, 1/48 scale, and highly detailed. The RailKing line is their semi-scale or O27 line. RailKing trains are built to the same rugged construction and engineering standards for quality, strength, and durability as the Premier line except that the level of detail is not as high, and they are, of course, slightly smaller than 1/48 scale.

Now that we have the basics down, let's get started with building a 4 x 8 train board.

There are several differences between O and O27 gauge trains. The first is that the rail height of O gauge track (on the left) is higher than O27 gauge rail height.

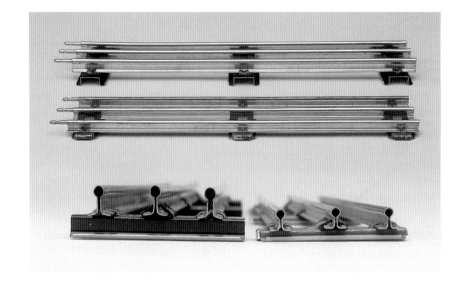

While O gauge trains are 1/48 scale models, O27 gauge trains are often a slightly smaller scale. This can be clearly seen on these two 40-foot boxcars, the larger being O gauge. The O27 gauge is a slightly smaller scale so that the locomotives and rolling stock will run on a 27-inch-diameter curve without jumping the track or derailing.

The traditional way to run power to standard O or O27 gauge track is by a simple "lock-on" device.

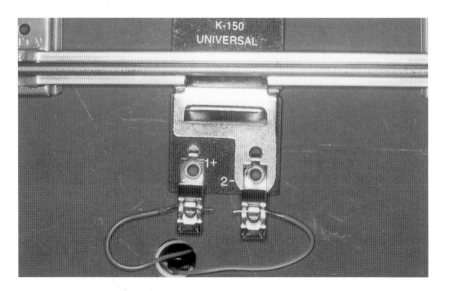

Track

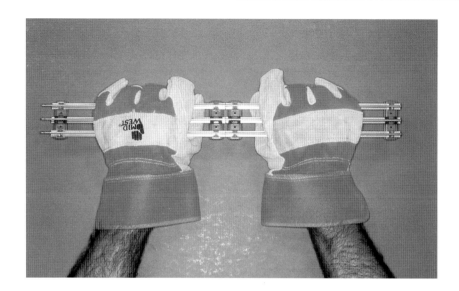

Standard O and O27 gauge track can cause small cuts on your hands, so it's not a bad idea to wear gloves when assembling traditional track.

This is how standard track looks on a train board. To deaden the sound of the trains and to improve the appearance of the track, roadbed is placed under the track, additional ties are inserted under the rails, and scale gravel is spread over the cork roadbed.

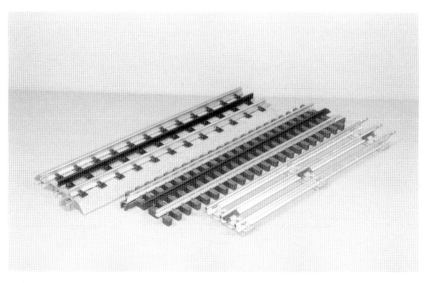

Standard track has been the mainstay for O and O27 gauge for nearly 100 years. Several manufacturers have introduced more scale-like track, but you still needed to lay down roadbed and add gravel. M.T.H. Electric Trains has introduced heavy-duty track (top left), which has the roadbed integrated into the track and can be used on just about any surface, including carpets.

This new 21st-century plug-and-play track system called "Real Trax" is available in several lengths of straight track, including 30-inch lengths. With these ready-made lengths you can build any layout without having to cut it to special lengths. Shown (from left) are the 10-, 5$\frac{1}{2}$-, 5-, 4$\frac{1}{4}$- and 3$\frac{1}{2}$-inch straight track lengths.

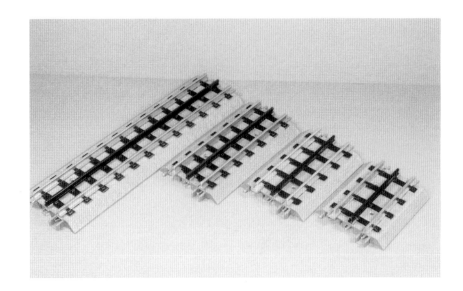

Real Trax also has various-diameter curves. Shown are the 72-, 42-, and 31-inch curves. Also available are 31- and 42-inch half curves.

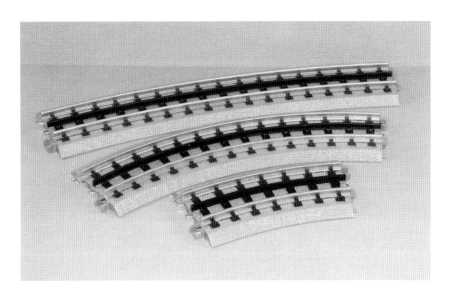

In keeping with the MTH concept of plug-and-play trains, all MTH track accessories, such as the uncoupler, are wired and ready to be plugged in.

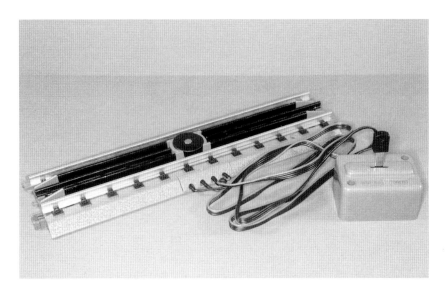

Even the bumpers are designed for plug-and-play. The little lights on the bumpers draw their power from the track.

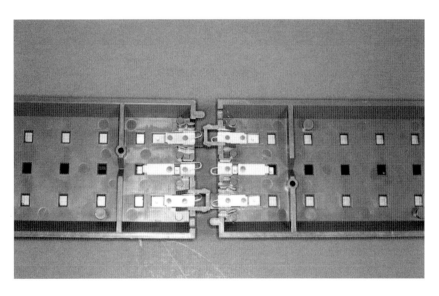

The underside of the Real Trax system has a positive snap-lock system, as well as heavy-duty brass connectors.

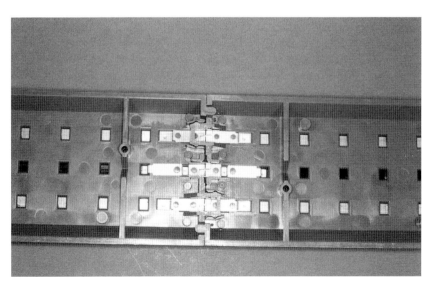

When the track is snapped together, the brass contacts are positively connected so that power is transferred along the individual track sections without the voltage drops that you typically experience with traditional track.

Track accessories can easily be plugged into the ready-made ports on the sides of the Real Trax system by simply snapping off one of the plug port covers. Each track length has at least one port.

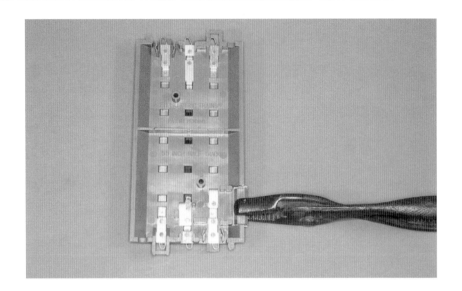

Since the Real Trax system has positive connection between track sections, only one lock-on is necessary, even for a relatively large layout. Traditional track would need several lock-ons to prevent voltage drops along the track.

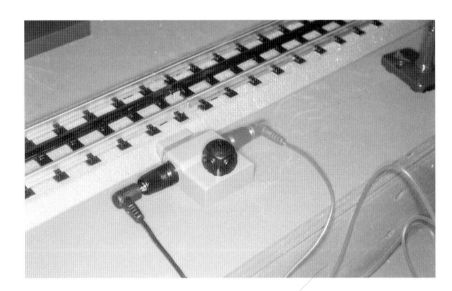

Switches

MTH's switches are beautifully designed and easy to install. The switches are powered from the track.

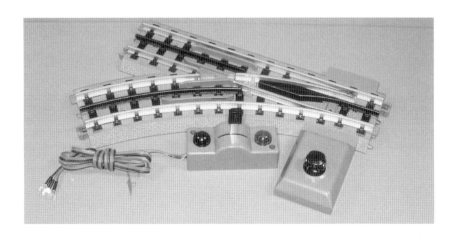

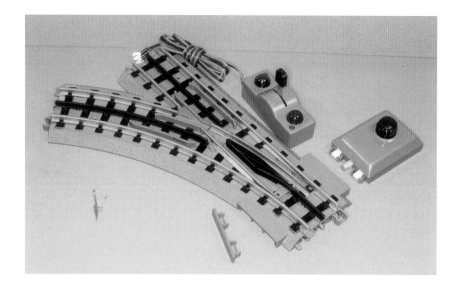

The motor that flips the track to the other route can be plugged into either side of the switch. There are no screws to mess with. Simply unplug it, pop out the cover on the other side, and then insert the motor pack into the new opening.

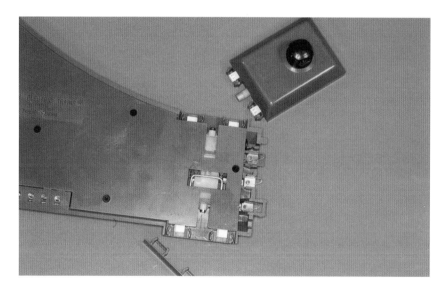

Here you can see the clean and simple design of the underside of the switches. There are no wires or screws to mess with, and here again, MTH designed their switches to be plug-and-play.

Transformers and Accessories

Several manufacturers, including MRC Corporation, make quality transformers for O and O27 gauge trains.

Many an American family has at least one old Lionel steam locomotive stuffed away in a closet that has been passed down from generation to generation. The MTH design engineers know this, as they are all trains lovers and they too have these family treasures.

MTH transformers are designed to run all types of modern locomotives, but they are also capable of powering those treasured old Lionel trains. MTH's standard Z-750 transformer provides power to run locomotives as well as accessories that are plugged into the Real Trax system.

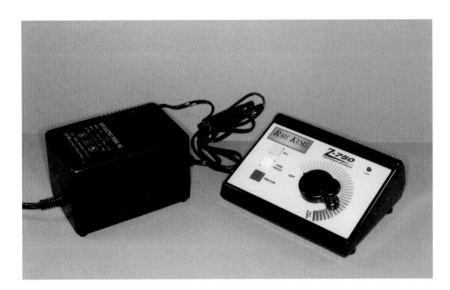

MTH's massive Z-4000 transformer is the ultimate in transformer design. It can run two trains at the same time and can be used to program just about any locomotive's digital sound system.

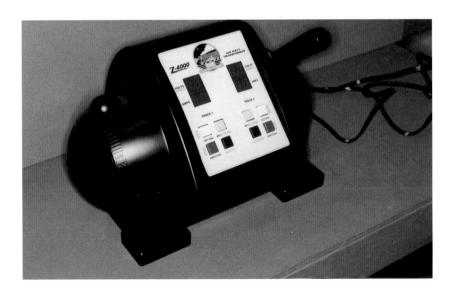

The MTH Z-4000 also has plenty of plugs for accessories requiring either 10 or 14 volts.

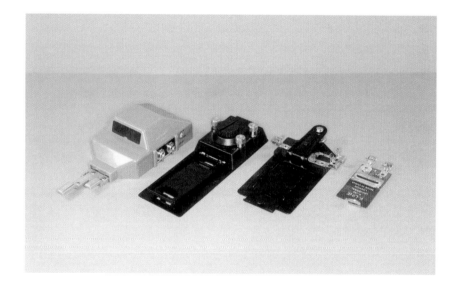

In keeping with their concept of plug-and-play trains, MTH has developed an infrared-sensor activation device (left) for accessories. This simple device plugs into the track and draws its power as well as power for the accessories directly from the track.

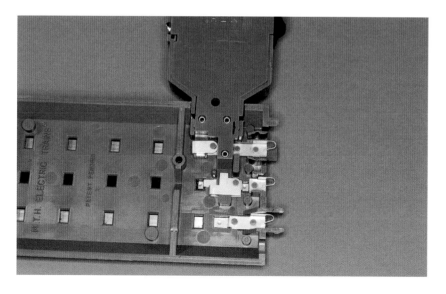

Here you can see the positive brass connectors designed to ensure that any device or accessory plugged into the track system will not experience voltage drop due to poor electrical contact.

MTH has a complete line of sturdy die-cast accessories from which to choose. Two favorites are the operating block signal and the crossing gate.

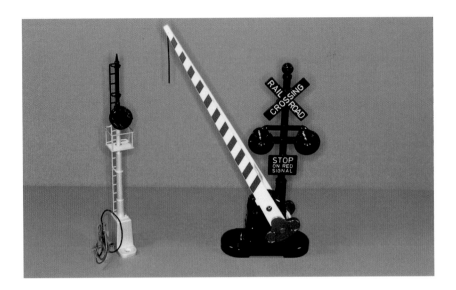

Structures

MTH's concept of plug-and-play trains also extends to structures, such as this two-story train station. This lighted structure is sturdily made of heavy plastic.

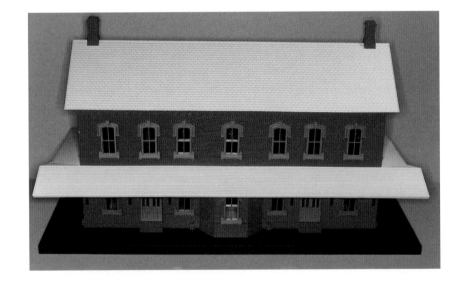

The ready-made train station above also comes with lighted covered platforms.

MTH offers several different styles of ready-made houses in a variety of colors.

These colorful and well-made structures are also lighted.

This switch tower is not only lighted, but it also has a detailed interior.

Here is a close-up of the tower's interior detail. Once the structure is wired for the interior lights, the detail will be easy to see.

MTH also makes several different styles and colors of die-cast metal lamps and street lights that are easy to hook up.

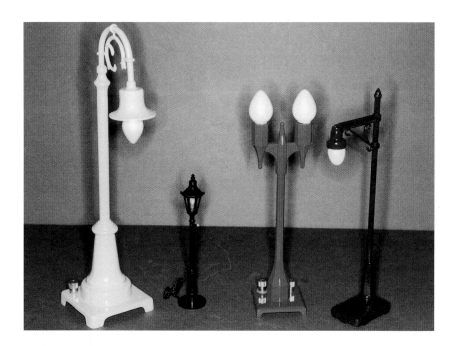

The MTH ready-made girder bridges and piers are well made and highly detailed. Their steel-arch bridge is 30 inches long.

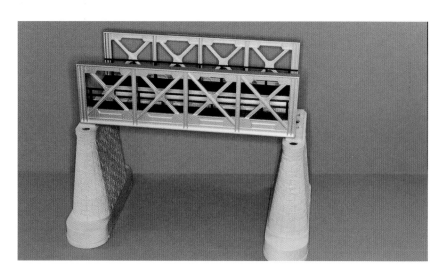

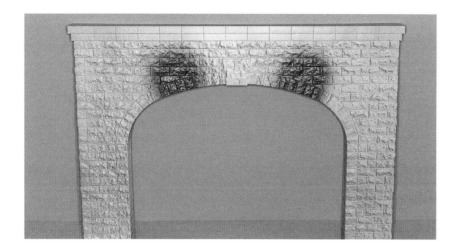

MTH makes both double and single tunnel portals for mountain scenery.

They even include the smoke stains you typically find along the tops of tunnel portals.

If you want to add structures that are not available from MTH, you can buy easy-to-assemble snap-together structures from several other manufacturers.

The MTH F-3A diesel locomotive is a popular engine, and it has a great horn. The pulling power of this locomotive is impressive.

Add a dummy A-unit (a B-unit is also available) and you have an impressive-looking setup.

Williams Electric Trains also makes well-built, reasonably priced, and reliable locomotives with great horns and good detail. This Canadian Pacific GP9 diesel locomotive is very colorful.

When buying rolling stock, always check to see that you are getting metal trucks and couplers.

Some trucks actually have springs so that they appear more realistic, like the ones on this boxcar.

The disks located on the bottoms of the couplers are for uncoupling. When the disk is located over an uncoupler track and the uncoupler is activated, the disk is drawn down, which opens the coupler.

Stock cars are my favorite type of rolling stock. They are available in many different colors and road names.

Boxcars can be either single-door or double-door.

The color combinations and road names available are almost endless.

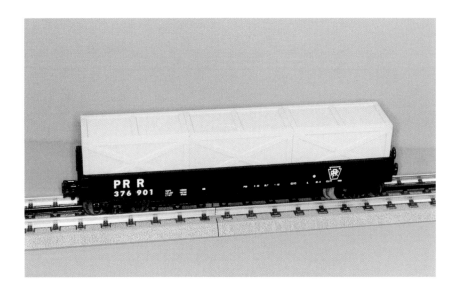

Children love gondolas, because they can load them up with all kinds of neat stuff.

Flatcars are also favorites, especially ones that come with die-cast metal accessories like automobiles, trucks, and road equipment.

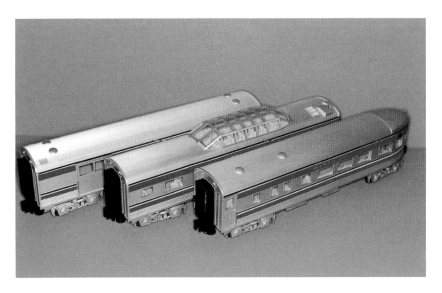

Passenger cars are also popular. All MTH cars have diaphragms between cars, undercarriage and interior detail, and lighted interiors.

While passenger cars of the same type may look alike, once they are painted differently with different road names added, they take on a special appearance.

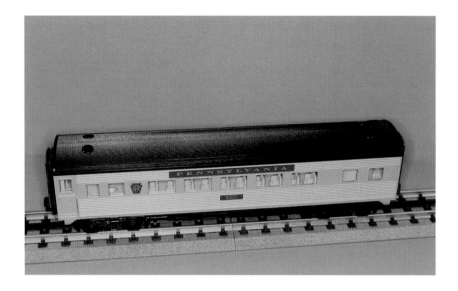

My favorite type of passenger cars are Pennsylvania Tuscan "Madison" cars.

These early-20th-century-style cars look great rolling down the track with a steam locomotive pulling them along.

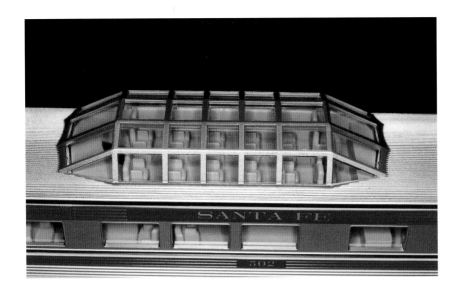

MTH pays special attention to the interior detailing of its passenger car line.

No train layout would be complete without a caboose. MTH cabooses are highly detailed, well built, and lighted so you can see the interior detail.

Repair

Simple modifications and maintenance will keep your MTH trains running for a lifetime. The B-unit for the F3 locomotive set has an external wire for the optional digital sound system. Since our locomotive has only a horn, we removed the external wire.

The first step in modifying the B-unit was to open it up and unplug the internal wiring.

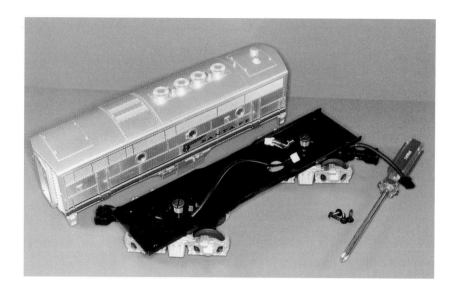

Next, we removed the wiring harness screw from the truck and pulled out the wire.

Now the B-unit looks better. We stored the wire and screw in a zip-lock bag and put the bag inside the B-unit's box so that we can reinstall it later.

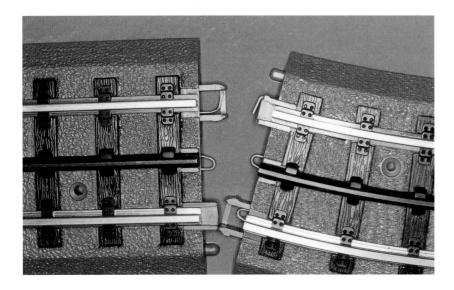

Sometimes the brass contacts on track sections clip to one another and get deformed when you pull the track sections apart.

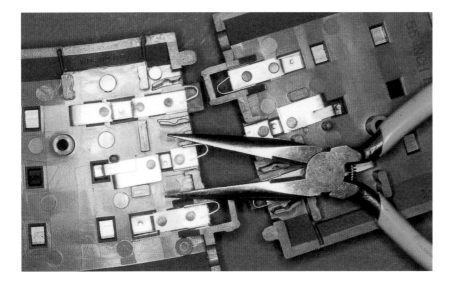

The simple fix is to use a set of needle-nose pliers to bend the brass contact back into shape.

Maintenance

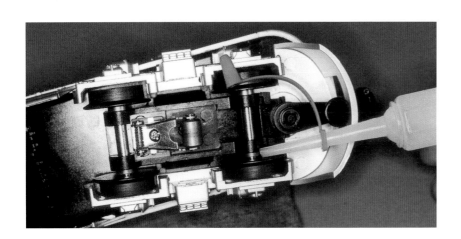

Diesel locomotive axles should be lubricated so the contact points between the wheel ends and the trucks will not wear out. While you should purchase train-lubricating oil, a light sewing-machine oil will do.

Lubricating the gears is an absolute must for all diesel locomotives. Small quantities applied to each gear work best.

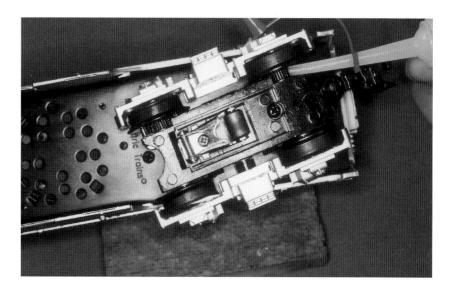

Steam locomotives have more gears than do diesels, and they require more lubricant and more-frequent applications.

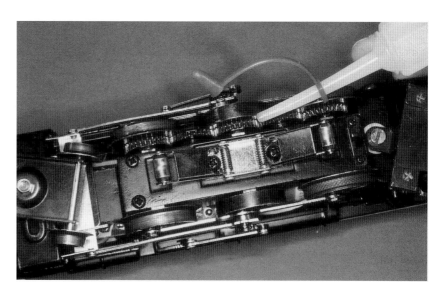

When lubricating the gears on a steam locomotive, do not forget to lubricate the bearings of the running gear and the drive rods.

One last tip on lubricating is to add a drop of oil to the axles of the pickup rollers of lighted freight and passenger cars.

Chapter Two

Benchwork

While you don't need to be an expert carpenter to build a well-constructed train board, some basic woodworking skills and tools are necessary to do the job right. You will need a tape measure, a 7-inch circular saw with a new blade, a drill, a Phillips-head screwdriver tip, a ½- to 1-inch wood drill bit, a carpenter's square, a hammer, a sanding block with 150-grit paper, a level, two wood clamps, a box of 3-inch deck screws, a pencil, and most important, safety glasses. If you do not have a circular saw, a drill, a level, or wood clamps, you can usually rent them for a nominal fee for a day. With these essential tools, you can build just about anything.

Wood supplies are pretty straightforward. To build the layout pictured in this book, you will need one 4 x 8-foot sheet of either ½-inch or ⅜-inch B/C grade plywood, a 15-inch-wide x 45-inch-long sheet of 12-inch B/C grade plywood for the control surface, and ten to twelve 2 x 4s, 8 feet long. The B/C grade means that the plywood has one side that is semi-finished and smooth. The 2 x 4s, which come in 8-foot lengths, will form the framing for the plywood as well as the legs. The best way to cut the smaller sheet of plywood for the control board is to have it done right there in the store.

When you go to your local building and wood supply store, check your wood selections carefully. Sweep your hands across the smooth plywood face to be sure there are no rough spots, cracks, splits, or bumps. The edges should be square and undamaged, and the plywood sheet should not be bowed or warped.

When selecting the 2 x 4s, don't be surprised if you have to sort through several layers of wood before you find 10 or 12 good ones. Always check the 2 x 4 for splits, knot holes, and warps. Also check all four planes—front, back, top, and bottom—to ensure that each length of lumber is straight. The easiest way to do this is pull a length out of the pile, lay one end on the floor, and sight down its entire length as you rotate the wood. Once you have selected your wood and assembled your tools, you are ready to get started.

The easy way to measure the plywood framing lengths is to position the 2 x 4 beneath the plywood and mark the lengths. Work on the 4-foot sides of the plywood first and be sure that one end of the 2 x 4 is butted up against the edge of the plywood.

When cutting the wood, prop up the end to be cut and use the carpenter's square as a guide for the circular saw. You may want to make several practice cuts. Then you'll get the feel of the saw as well as the placement and adjustment of the carpenter's square so that the blade of the saw will cut along the marked line. If you use a carpenter's square to guide your saw, you will have a perfect cut every time. Since circular saws kick out a lot of sawdust and slivers, it's important that you wear those safety glasses. After each cut run the sanding block across the cut edges to smooth them out.

Once you have cut both ends, secure them in place, making sure the smooth side of the plywood is facing you. I like to use 3-inch deck screws. The screws hold the wood together tighter and stronger, and if you decide to dismantle the board some day you just simply back out the screws. Nails do too much damage to the wood when you try to remove them.

Position both lengths beneath the plywood edges and then, using that time-and-wrist-saving Phillips-head screwdriver-equipped drill, carefully screw one piece in place. Then go on to the other side and screw the other 2 x 4 in place. Drive screws into both ends, about

an inch from the edge of the plywood, and then space more screws 6 to 8 inches apart. Once the ends are done, measure the lengths, which should be approximately 7 feet 9 inches long, and then secure these lengths to the plywood. To secure the ends of the 2 x 4s to each other, run two screws at each of the four ends into the wood. This will really stiffen the frame.

The next step is to add additional support across the 4-foot width of the plywood to stiffen it. I recommend that you add three additional lengths of 2 x 4s to the underside of the framing. To do this, flip the plywood over, mark the three locations where the wood will go on the frame, and then place a length of 2 x 4 over the first location and mark the length. Since the control board (added later) is 45 inches long, the two outer lengths of additional framing also need to be this width apart because you will attach the framing of the control board to them. When you measure the three locations on the frame, be sure you start from the same end for the front and back locations. Cut these lengths one at a time, and secure them in place with two screws at each end.

Once all three lengths are in place, flip the plywood over again and mark the locations of the screws that hold these three lengths in place on the surface of the plywood. Use the edges of the level to run a line that connects the marked locations, and then add a few screws to each length. Be sure to measure the locations of the screws because you will need to mark them on the underside.

Again turn the plywood over, mark the locations of the screws on the three interior frames so that the drill bit will not hit them, and then drill some holes into the three lengths of wood with your large-bore drill bit. To prevent the wood from splintering on the opposite side of where you are drilling, clamp an additional piece of wood to this surface. These holes will channel the electrical wires, help secure them, and also prevent them from dangling down.

Now you are ready to make and attach the legs. Cut eight equal lengths of 2 x 4s for the legs. A good length for legs is approximately 36 inches. This height is great for children between the ages of 6 and 9 because the height of the train board will be just about level with their eyes. This is also a good height for sitting on a stool at the control board. To ensure that all the legs are cut the same length, cut one length, mark it as the master, and then use it to mark the additional lengths so that all the leg lengths are the same.

Assemble the four legs by using several screws to attach two lengths together on an edge so that the leg forms an L. Be sure that the ends and edges are butted together. To make the screw assembly easier, place another length of wood under the other side so that the 2 x 4s form a box. Once the legs are assembled, position them one by one onto the inside ends of

the frame. Use a level to be sure they are straight, and then screw them in place. Between the legs (and on the 4-foot side of the train board) add a length of wood along the frame. This will provide a flush surface for the angled brace. To stiffen the legs, cut lengths of 2 x 4s at 45-degree angles using the carpenter's square and screw one into each leg and then into the frame. Each length should be about 24 to 30 inches long. One angle support for each leg usually does the trick.

Now you are ready for the last step, which is to add the control board. Cut two lengths of 2 x 4s approximately 36 inches long, and then cut six lengths 7 inches long. Mark 21 inches on each of the 36-inch lengths, and then position them onto the outer two underside frames of the train board so that the lengths of wood are stacked on top of one another and the marks line with the outer edge of the train board frame. There should be exactly 15 inches of wood sticking

out from the face of the train board frame, which is also the exact width of the piece of plywood that you had cut for the control board surface. Position the 7-inch lengths of wood onto the sides of the stacked 2 x 4s. You should have two on one side, one on the other.

Next, screw them into place, being sure to use four screws in each 7-inch length. Once this is done, comlete the framing on the control board by adding the front and rear frame members. These should be 42 inches long.

Next, position the control board top and screw it into place. Once you decide where you want to position the transformer, accessory controls, and switch controls, you can drill access holes in the control board surface for the wires. Now you are ready for the last step, painting the train and control board surfaces. I recommend a medium- to dark-green paint, which will help blend the surface of the train board into the scenery that you will add later.

Tabletop and Framing

Having carefully selected the wood you'll need, begin by placing 2 x 4s under both sides to balance the plywood and to provide for an accurate mark. Also mark which 2 x 4 goes where, as sometimes plywood sheets can have slightly different dimensions.

After cutting (wearing safety glasses, of course) the 2 x 4s to your marked lengths, position the cut 2 x 4s under the 4-foot ends of the plywood and mark the locations for the screws.

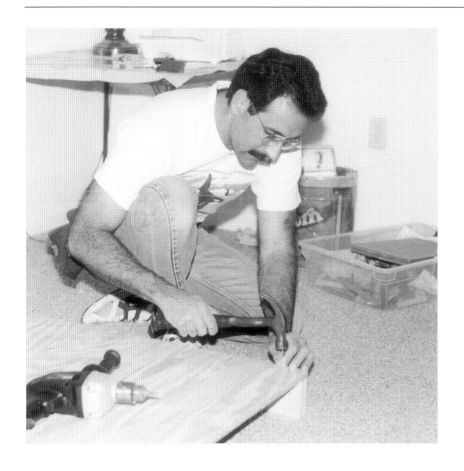

Use 3-inch deck screws to secure the plywood to the frame. Start the deck screws by hammering them slightly into place.

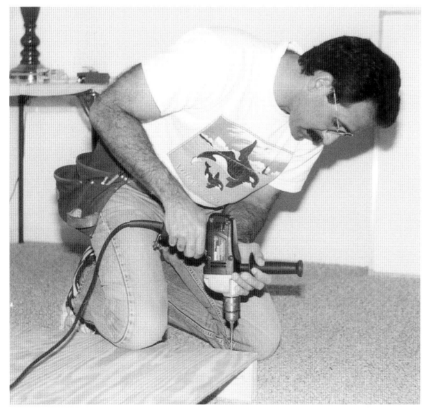

Use a drill with a Phillips-head attachment to turn the screws into place. The end screws should be an inch or so from the ends, and the rest should be about 8 inches apart.

To cut and fit the longer sides of the frame, which should measure out close to 7 feet 9 inches, turn the plywood over, position the 2 x 4s, mark and cut the lengths, and then fit them in place. To secure the longer 2 x 4s in place, drive two screws through each end of the 2 x 4s, thus securing the frame together. Now you can flip the train board over again and add screws along the plywood surface to really secure the plywood to the frame.

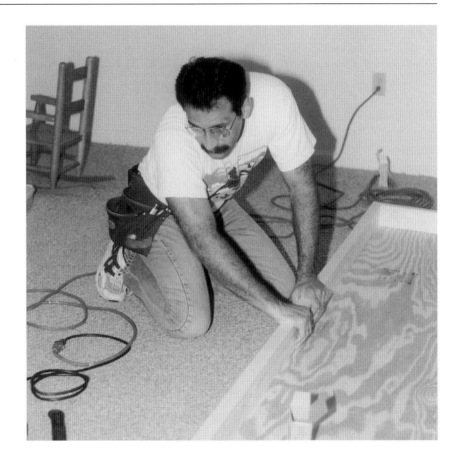

To complete the frame, flip the train board over again and add three additional interior lengths. Be sure to mark the locations of these interior frame members on the ends of the outer frame so that you can transfer the marked locations to the plywood surface. Since the control board length is 45 inches, the distance between the outer faces of the two end frame members needs to be this distance.

Use a level to connect the marks for the interior frames along the surface of the plywood. Measure locations for the screws along the lines and then screw them into place. Now you will have a strong train board.

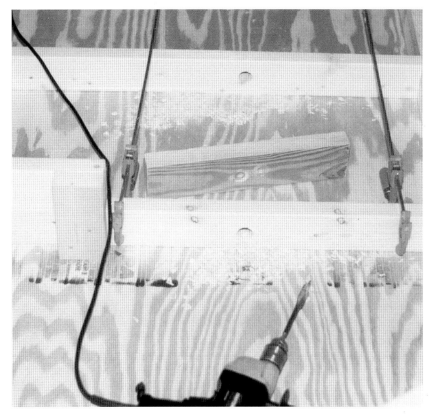

To facilitate and help hide the electrical wiring, drill holes in the interior frames using a large wood bit. To prevent the wood from splintering where the drill comes out, clamp an additional piece of wood on the back side of the frame where you plan to drill.

Here the first leg (assembled by securing together two 36-inch lengths of 2 x 4 at a 90-degree angle) is being positioned. Once the leg is perfectly perpendicular, screw it into place with 3-inch deck wood screws.

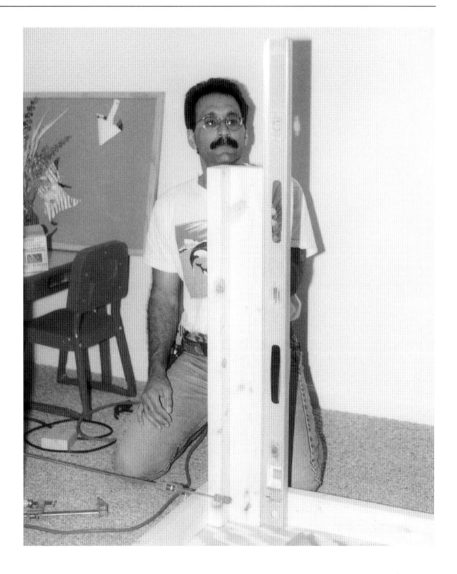

At this point angle braces, cut at 45-degree angles at both ends, have been added. This end is now done, and pretty soon it will be time to add the control board. Note that in order for the 45-degree braces to sit flush against the frame you have to add an additional length of wood to the back side of the frame.

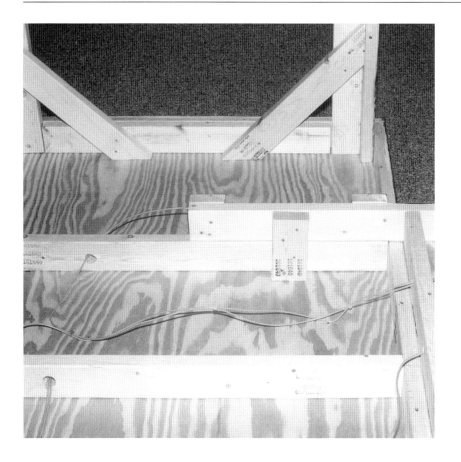

Using the instructions in the introduction to the chapter, assemble the control panel and attach it to the table. Note how the control board frame is attached to the interior frame members with 7-inch lengths of 2 x 4. This is why I stated earlier that the interior frame members needed to be 45 inches apart.

The control panel and train board surfaces have been painted dark green, and we're now ready to lay out track and run some trains. The construction techniques used to build this train board are very simple, yet the board is so strong and stable that you can stand on it.

Chapter Three
Track Layout and Wiring

Once you have your train board completed, you are ready to start playing with some track, switches, locomotives, and rolling stock. Before you settle on any particular track plan, try several different configurations. While your options are somewhat limited because of the size of the train board and the size of O gauge trains, you can pack a lot onto a 4 x 8 layout. Sketch a layout or just lay some track and switches on the board. Move them around until you come up with a combination you like. Keep this first layout simple with only two or three switches.

When you've arrived at what you believe to be the THE plan, drill small holes through the plywood for the switch wires and run some wire to them. Position the lock-on near the transformer, power up the track, and check the switches. Since the switches draw their power from the track, all you have to do is hook up three wires for each switch and you are ready to play.

Once you get a feel for the transformer and the locomotive's response to a variety of power settings, practice throwing the switches as a train approaches. When you and your children are comfortable with the process, you are ready to advance to a more complicated layout with more switches.

After you have experienced several different track configurations, you will naturally gravitate to a favorite one. When you've gotten to that point, lay out the track and switch, flip the switch motors where necessary, drill any switch-wiring holes that are needed, and plug in your trusty lock-on. Manually test the switches, fix any fluttering or consistent throw problems (page 48), and then test the trains on the track.

Once you are satisfied that the layout works, decide where you want accessories and infrared sensors. The sensors need to be plugged into the same side of the track as the lock-on. What I mean by this is that if the lock-on is connected to the outer part of the track, the outside and middle rails will be electrically wired. Conversely, if the lock-on is connected to the inside of the track, the inside and middle rails will be electrically wired. For the sensor to work properly, it must be plugged into the lock-on-powered rails so that it can draw power to run the sensor and the accessory.

Before we go on, let's take a moment to discuss why O and O27 gauge trains have three rails. The three-rail standard was set by the Lionel Corporation when they introduced electric trains almost 100 years ago. Having three rails simplified the electrical wiring for all the working accessories that Lionel planned to make. By powering only the inner rail and one other rail, the dead rail became the switch for all the accessories. Because the wheels on trains are metal, they make electrical contact between the inner and outer rail. Locations for accessories required that you isolate a length of rail so that it did not have electrical contact with the rest of the track. As the train passed over this length of rail, the wheels provided electrical power to that isolated length, thereby turning on any accessories connected to it.

The wiring required to do all this is perhaps not as simple as this explanation, which is why MTH designed their plug-and-play accessories and track. The plug-and-play concept takes advantage of the three-rail design for activating accessories, but without the headaches of wiring, thanks to their infrared sensor and accessories designed to draw low voltage from the track.

I settled on a modified large oval with two curves at one end, a reversing loop, two sidings for storage of additional rolling stock, one uncoupler, and six switches—three left and three right. A reversing loop allows you to literally reverse the direction of the train by stopping the last car of the train just past the switch, throwing the switch and then backing the train completely through the section of track, and then throwing the switch at the other end of the track. When the train goes forward again, it will be running in the opposite direction. Reversing loops help your children practice running and stopping trains as well as throwing switches. An uncoupler allows you to remotely uncouple rolling stock from each other or the locomotive. Here you and your children get practice positioning the trucks directly over the uncoupler to disconnect them.

For accessories I chose two crossing gate signals, one block signal, three different types of street lamps, and four lighted buildings—two houses, a switch tower, and a station. Once the track was positioned on the train board, I placed all the accessories in their approximate locations both to check the fit and to see how they would look on the layout. I also marked the locations of any infrared sensors and popped out the tabs on the track for these locations. I did not secure any of the accessories at this time.

That's part of the next chapter. For now, let's concentrate on getting the track laid out, adjusted, wired, and secured to the train board.

Once you are satisfied with the layout, it's time to screw down the track. Track and switches have recessed holes in them for screws. Use a wood punch to set a starter hole in the plywood, and then set the screws in place. The best screws are no. 4, ⅜-inch panhead zinc-plated, available in just about any hardware store. It's not necessary to place a screw in every hole; one per section is plenty. Once the track is in place, drill holes for the switch and lock-on wiring.

Next, decide where on the control panel you want the switch controllers, line them up, mark holes for the wiring, and then drill the holes. Be sure you leave enough room between the controllers and the edge of the control panel so you can label the controllers and still have room for a diagram of the layout, complete with corresponding numbers for the switches. Secure the switch controllers with screws, and run the wire from each controller through the corresponding holes in the control panel. The holes for the screws on the switch controllers are very small; Atlas sells bags of O gauge track screws that fit perfectly.

Since the wires attached to the controllers are not going to be long enough to reach all the switches, you will need to lengthen them. The easiest way to do this is to add electrical screw terminal strips under the train board and make longer wire lengths to reach the turnouts. These terminal screw strips, which come in various lengths, can be found in any electronics supply store, such as Radio Shack. To keep things neat and organized, screw the terminal strips into the inside of the train board frame just behind the control panel where the switch controllers are located.

The next step is to cut individual lengths of wire that will reach from the switch to the terminal strip. To ensure that you do not mix up the wiring, use the same colors for these new lengths as those supplied with the switch controllers: black, red, and green. You can use either solid

wire or stranded wire, but I like to use stranded because it is more flexible and easier to work with. Atlas sells spools of stranded 20 gauge wire and solderless wire clips, both of which are designed specifically for model railroading. For this particular layout you will need two spools of red, two of black, two of green, and several bags of solderless clips. To make the wire lengths and use the solderless clips, you will also need a wire stripper/crimper. Here again, this handy tool can be found in Radio Shack stores. One more item you will need is small plastic tie strips, which can be found at just about any hardware store.

Work with one switch at a time and measure each group of wire lengths separately, strip the ends, and then add the solderless connectors. Next, take several tie strips, secure the three wires together with the tie strips so they are bundled, and then cut the excess tie strip end. Usually three or four strips are all that is needed for each wire bundle. Run the wire bundle through the plywood to the switch,

hook the wires to the switch's screw posts, and then run the wires back to a terminal strip. When running the wires under the train board, be sure to run them through the holes that you drilled into the framing.

Connect the wires from the switch to the terminal strip, and then connect the wires from the controller to the same terminal strip screws, being sure to match wire colors. The switch controllers should be grouped together so you can control the switches as a locomotive approaches them. Wire one switch at a time and wire switches that are close together, working from the locations farthest away from the control panel to the nearest.

The excess wire from the switch controllers should also be bundled using tie strips so that the underside of the train board does not start to look like spaghetti. Neatness and organization count in wiring a train board, because if you have an electrical problem it will be easy to trace the wires if they are individually bundled, tie-stripped together, and tagged.

Once you have completed all the switch wiring, hook up the wires for the transformer, and test the track and switches. Once all the turnouts check out, you are ready to run some trains. Practice working the locomotive around the track, especially the reversing loop, and also practice throwing the switches as the locomotive approaches. One last thing you can do is to paint the shiny heads on the screws holding down the track. I recommend Testors primer, which is a gray color and comes in either a water-based or enamel mixture. Testors paints can be found in any hobby store.

Adding Switches

After temporarily placing track on the table and running trains for a while, it's time to add some switches to your layout. Switches are easy to install and wire. It's helpful to remember that the interior curved rails are not electrically connected to anything. This is because these inner rails are the sensors for the nonderailing feature on the switches.

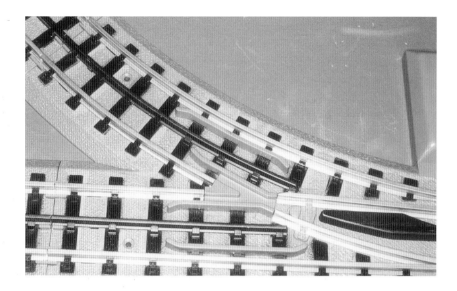

A look at the underside of this switch reveals there are no electrical connectors for the inner rails.

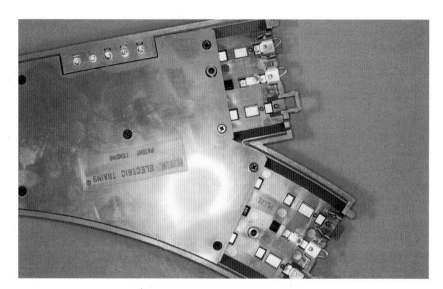

The inner rail on this switch is the correct length, which is slightly shorter so that it will not touch the adjoining rail.

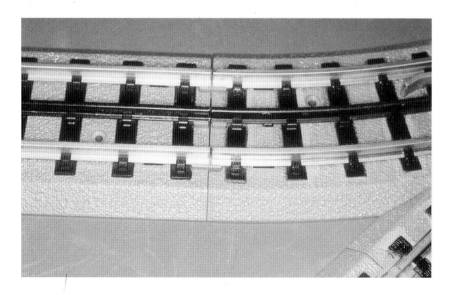

Simple Switch Fixes

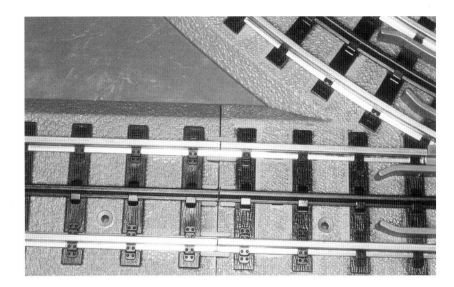

The inner rail of this switch is slightly off and is touching the adjoining rail. As a result, the electrical motor for the switch will flutter or constantly be thrown in one direction.

A simple fix for this problem is to insert a small piece of clear plastic from the switch packaging between the two rail ends.

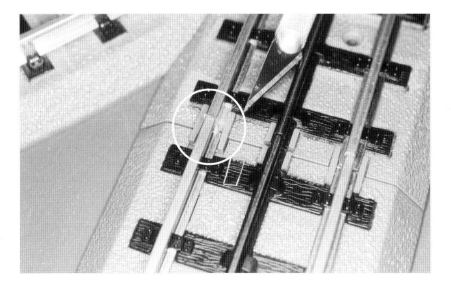

Use a sharp hobby knife to trim plastic from the inside of the rail so that it will not interfere with the wheels of the locomotive or the rolling stock.

Another easy problem to fix is an overly sensitive switch controller. Simply remove the controller cover and bend the electrical contacts away from one another.

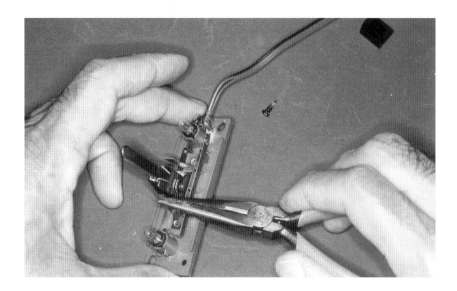

Track Plan Ideas

Once children get a feel for the locomotive, it's time to add some switches. I have modified the oval by adding what is referred to as a reversing loop. This give the kids practice backing up, throwing the switches, and using the locomotive's E-unit.

Here is another variation on the oval. This time I removed the reversing loop and added a smaller oval with a siding for storage of rolling stock.

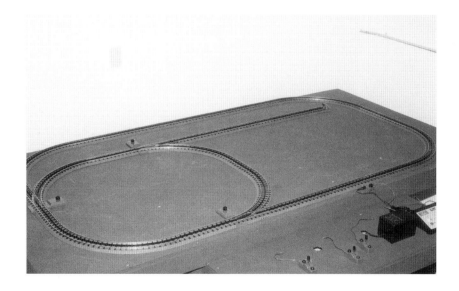

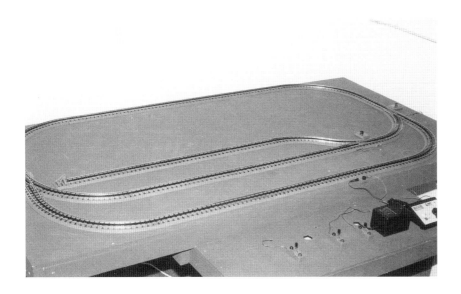

Still another variation on the oval with a long siding. Children seem to master throwing the switches quicker than adults, so now it's time to make a more complicated lay-out with more switches.

Thanks to M.T.H. Electric Trains' design for the low power draw of the switch motors, you do not need an additional trans-former to power them. The switches draw their power directly from the track. Wiring the controllers for the switches is also very easy.

Final Configuration

Here's the track design we decided to go with. It will appear throughout the rest of the book. There are three right- and three left-hand switches, 12 lengths of 31-inch curved track, 12 lengths of 10-inch straight track, 2 lengths of 4½-inch track, 4 lengths of 3½-inch straight track, 6 lengths of 5½-inch straight track, two bumpers, one uncoupler, and one lock-on.

Before I screwed down the track, I positioned all the accessories onto the layout to check their locations and to be sure that they would not interfere with one another or the track. I powered up the track and ran a locomotive around the layout. Kids like lots of lights and motion—come to think of it, so do adults!

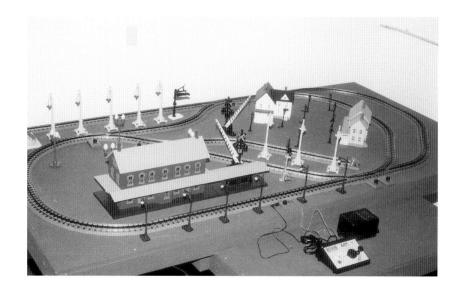

Attach the Track and Switches

To secure the track to the train board, use a punch to start a hole in the plywood.

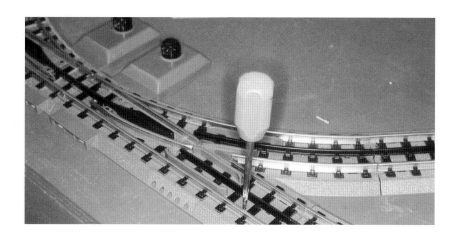

Use no. 4 ⁵⁄₈-inch panhead screws to secure the track to the plywood. You don't need to place a screw into every hole on each length of track; just add enough screws to hold the track in place.

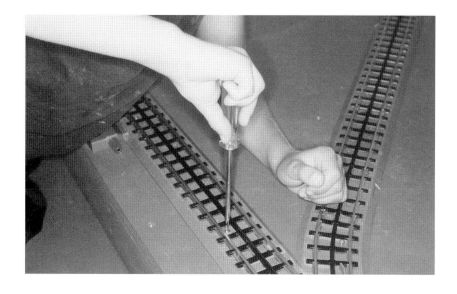

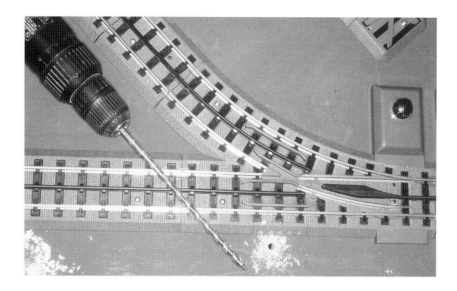

The next step is to drill small holes into the plywood for the switch wiring.

Position the switch controllers on the control panel, mark the locations for the wires, and then drill holes in the panel.

Wiring Supplies

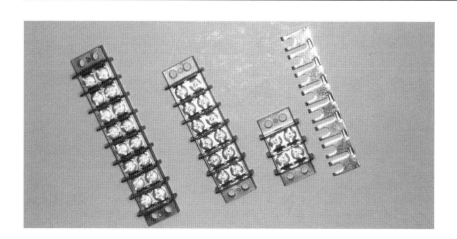

Since some of the switches are farther away from the controllers than the lengths of provided wire, you will need some simple electrical supplies to make extra wire lengths. You will also need terminal screw strips and terminal jumpers similar to the ones shown here.

You will need additional wire. Use 20 gauge wire that is either stranded or solid. One advantage of stranded wire is its flexibility. For larger layouts, you'll want to use solid wire of a larger gauge (though smaller number).

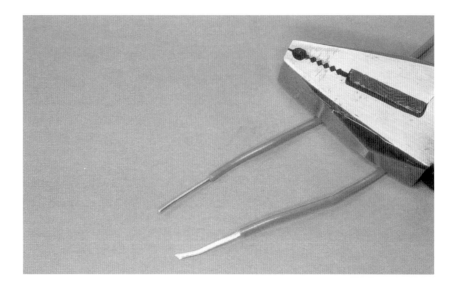

Atlas sells spools of stranded 20 gauge colored wire that is specifically designed for model railroading. Almost every hobby shop carries it.

You will also need solderless connectors and a wire stripper. The solderless connectors can be purchased at Radio Shack along with the wire stripper/crimper. Atlas also sells solderless connectors.

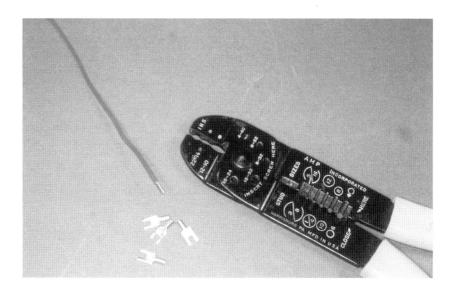

"Lengthening" the Switch Wires

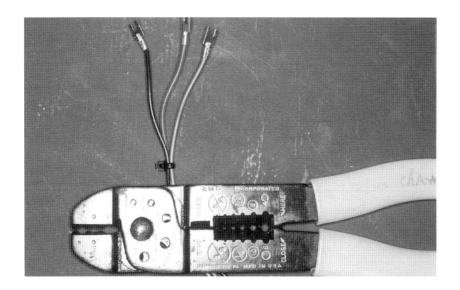

Measure the distance from the switches to where the terminal strips will be located. Make bundles of wire cut to a little more than that length using red, black, and green wire. Bundle them together with plastic tie strips.

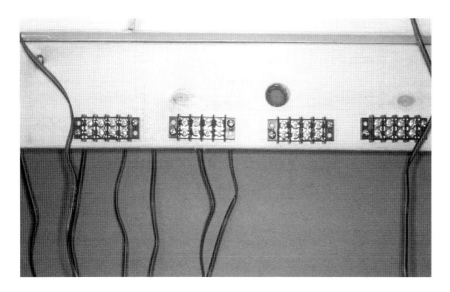

Here, four screw terminal strips have been attached to the back side of the train board framing just behind the control panel and close to the switch controls.

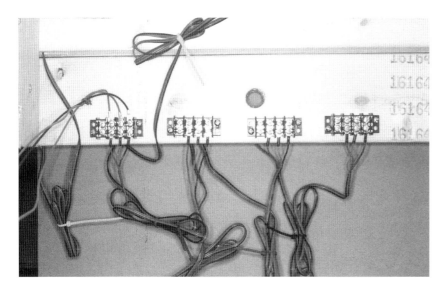

This photo shows that the wires that come with the switch controls have been attached to the terminal screws, and the first wire bundle set for a switch has been added. Connect the other bundles in the same way.

The bundled-wire colors should match the original control-wire colors so that there is no chance of a mix-up. This also makes it easy for children to do the screw terminal hookups.

To help keep the wire bundles tucked under the table, you can buy plastic wire holders and screw them into the underside framing.

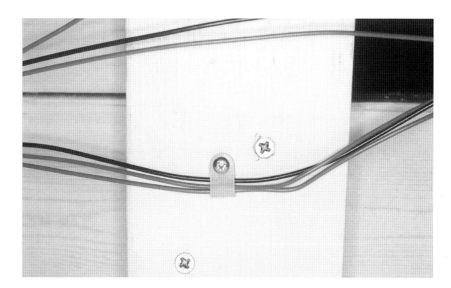

The great thing about terminal strips is that you can use them just about anywhere. I cut one length of wire bundle too short, so I made another short length and simply connected them using a terminal strip.

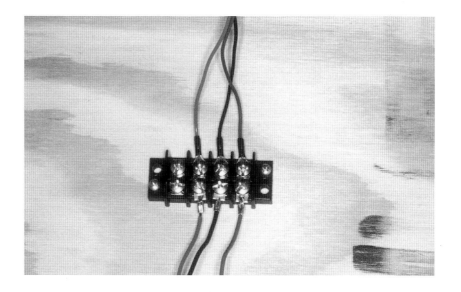

Completing the Wiring

Here the wire bundle ends are attached to the screw posts on the switch. Be sure that the brass jumper (at right) is not removed, as this is the internal jumper that tells the tiny motor inside the turnout to get its power from the track instead of an external source.

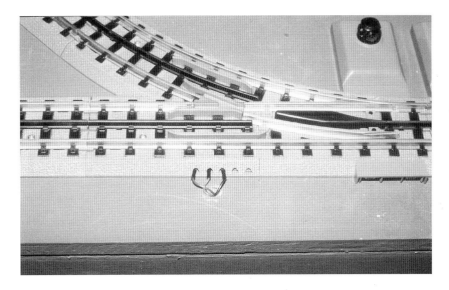

This switch is now wired and ready to go. Neatness counts—especially on top of the layout!

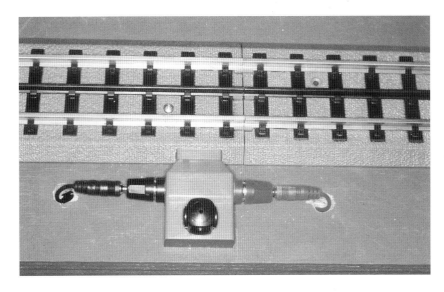

Note how the lock-on wires are connected. There is no excess wire on top of the plywood.

Test the Wiring

Now that all the turnouts are wired, it's time to test them. The standard Z-750 transformer provides more than enough power to run the switches. Turn on the transformer and start flipping controller handles to check your wiring.

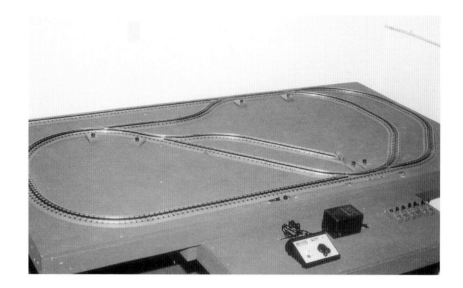

Note how neat the control panel looks. With the controllers all in a row, labeling them will be easy.

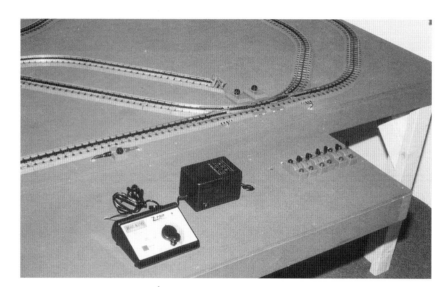

Once you're sure all the switches are operational, it's time to run a train.

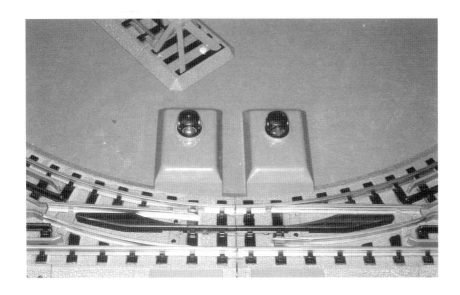

The switches have green (straight route) and red (diverging or curved route) lights so that you can identify which way the switch is thrown. These lights correspond to the ones on the switch controllers. To change the light color, simply pop out the plastic cover and rotate it.

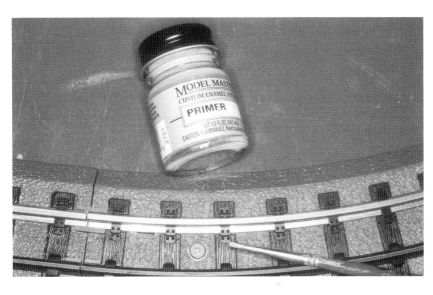

One simple "dress-up" project is to paint the heads on the screws to camouflage them.

Now that's a smile worth waiting for! After helping Dad build the train board, lay the track, and wire the turnouts, Thomas has his reward.

Chapter Four

Adding Accessories to Your Layout

In the previous chapter we positioned the accessories on the train board to ensure that everything fit. Now it is time to start wiring them. I started with the MTH ready-built structures. When you add accessories that do not draw their power from the track, such as lighted structures or streetlights, you need an alternate power source. Several manufacturers make small power supplies that provide power for various accessories. Since I plan to expand the size of my layout in the future, I purchased an MTH Z-4000 transformer. The Z-4000 packs a lot of power, it can run two trains, it is designed to program the sound effects available in locomotives, and it has terminal distribution clips for 10 and 14 volts.

Lighted structures

To get started, mark the locations of the ready-made structures by positioning them and drawing their base outlines onto the train board. I drilled holes in the center of the outline for the wiring so I could pass the wires from the buildings down through the track board and underneath the layout. The undersides of the structures have electrical clips, so all you have to do is strip about ⅛ inch off the ends of the wires and clip them into place. When running the wires beneath the train board, be sure to leave about 6 inches of slack in the wire so that you can lift the structure off the board to get underneath it.

Since I planned to have all the lights for the ready-made structures controlled by one switch, I installed two terminal screw strips under the train board to distribute power to all the structures. To simplify the distribution of power for each strip, I purchased metal clips that attach to the screws and distribute the power to all the terminals that are connected together by the metal clip. I like to use red and black wire for these types of hookups: red is the hot lead and black is the cool lead, or ground.

Measure each length of wire for each structure separately, bundle them with plastic tie strips, add solderless connectors, and run the wire bundles through the holes drilled into the underside of the train board frame. Sometimes the wire crimper does not crimp the solderless connector tight enough, so always check each lead by giving each solderless connector a slight tug after you crimp it. If it is loose, simply crimp it in another location. This usually does the trick.

Once all the structures are wired to the terminal strips, make another two-wire bundle to run from the terminal strip to the switch located on the control board. For the switch I used an Atlas connector block. Each connector block has three switches, and the blocks are designed so you can link them together. This allows you to have as many switches as you want with electrical power distributed automatically throughout all the switches. The power from the transformer is attached to the leads on the left side of the connector block, and there are two screw terminal posts for each switch. I attached the wires from the terminal strips of the structures to the first two screw terminals of the Atlas connector, turned on the transformer, and flipped the switch to check the lights.

Lamp posts

As I mentioned earlier, I chose four different types of lighted lamp posts. I chose single-bulb, cream-colored, die-cast gooseneck lamps for the long track siding; pea green, double-bulb teardrop die-cast street lights for the train station parking

lot; and dark green, single-bulb die-cast streetlights for the train station platform. I also added black single-bulb lamps for the streetlights. Some of the die-cast lamps have screw terminal posts with holes drilled into them so that you can either push the wire through the hole or wrap the wire around the terminal post.

I wired up all the lamps the same as the structure lights. I attached two terminal strips to the underside of the train board, added the electrical distribution clips, and then wired the lamps to the terminal strip. To save time and stranded wire, I used standard telephone wire, which you can also buy at Radio Shack. This wire has four leads—red, black, green, and yellow. They are solid copper wire and are encased in flexible plastic insulation. I stripped about 6 inches of insulation from each side of a length of wire, and since I needed only red and black, I cut off the other two. I then proceeded to wire the die-cast lamps just like the structure lights. The die-cast street lamps were all wired together and hooked up to the second switch on the Atlas connector.

The black street lamps with the thin wires attached required an extra step. Since the wires that were attached to the lamps were very thin, they needed a special connector to attach them to the telephone wires I was using. I found the solution at Radio Shack, which sells small splice connectors that are quick and easy to use. To use these splice connectors, cut the ends off the wire, slip the wire ends into the holes on the flat end of the splice connector, and crimp the disk on the face of the connector with a pair of pliers. The disk has thin metal strips on the inside that will cut through the insulation of the wire and create an electrical contact between them. Once the wires were spliced, I ran them back to another set of terminal strips and then connected the terminal strips to the third switch on the Atlas connector.

Uncoupler

Since I wanted to have an uncoupler at the beginning of the long siding, I removed the length of track attached to the switch and replaced it with an uncoupler. Like the switches, uncouplers come completely wired to their controllers. The uncoupler was too far away to attach the wire directly, so I had to make a four-wire bundle and add a terminal strip to the underside of the train board. (I had to do the same thing with the switch wiring.) Since the wires were already attached to the uncoupler, and three of them were black and one was brown, I attached small lengths of masking tape to the wires and labeled them and the terminal screws they were attached to: 1 through 4.

Then I removed the labeled wires from the screw posts on the uncoupler, attached the uncoupler control to the control panel, and ran the wires from the uncoupler control under the train board to the terminal strip. I used the telephone wire to connect the terminal strip to the uncoupler. As I attached each of the four wires I wrote down which color from the telephone wire was attached to which numbered wire from the controller. I then attached the colored wires to their corresponding locations on the uncoupler. I could have simply attached the controller closer to the uncoupler, but I wanted all the controls to be located at the control panel.

Crossing gates and block signal

To wire the crossing gates and the block signal, I inserted the three infrared sensors into the track locations where I had

removed the pop-out tabs from the track. One was located at the end of the long siding, and two were located at both ends of the reversing loop so that the crossing gates could be activated from a train entering the reversing loop from either direction. Just like the lock-on, the infrared sensors simply plug into the track. Next I drilled holes in the train board for the wires going to the sensors and holes for the two crossing gates and the block signal.

I added a terminal strip to the underside of the train board and made four bundles of wires for the crossing gate hookups. One bundle went from the terminal strip to the crossing gate, and one bundle went to each infrared sensor. I used black and red wires to ensure that I would not cross the polarity of the electrical current coming from the sensors. To wire the crossing gate to the correct terminal screws on the infrared sensors, I simply followed the sensor and crossing gate instructions. The sensors are designed so that you can hook them up together, and each sensor can power several accessories.

Once the crossing gates were

hooked up, I tested the sensors and adjusted them. This is important, as the sensors have two adjustments. The first is the range adjustment—which I recommend you set to low so that only the oncoming train will activate the sensor. The range is from approximately 1½ to 14 inches. The other sensor is the delay adjustment, which simply sets the time delay for the accessory.

Next I wired the block signal and again set the adjustments on the infrared sensor. The block signal will stay red as long as there are trains occupying the track siding. When the sensor detects that the trains are no longer there, the block signal will temporarily turn to yellow and then to green. The light on the block signal will stay green until the siding is occupied again, at which time it turns red.

The last thing I did was type up some labels for the Atlas connector switches and some reminders for my boys to help them run the trains. I also drew a diagram of the layout, numbered the switches on the diagram, and placed corresponding numbers on the individual switch controllers. This made it easy for all of us to know which switch to throw as a train approached.

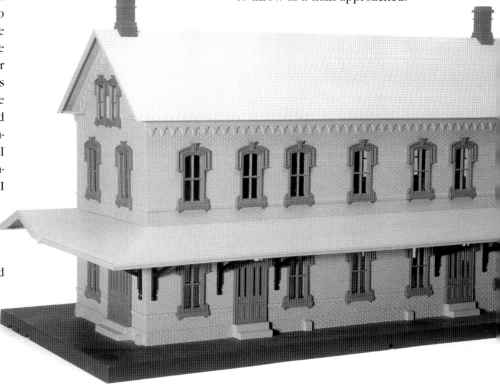

To wire the MTH ready-made structures, position them on the train board and run a pencil around their bases to mark their locations.

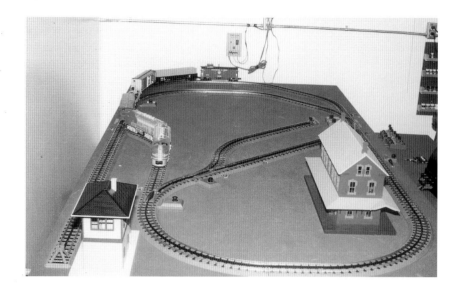

Next, drill holes into the plywood through which you will run the wire for the lighting.

You will need to make two wire bundles for all the lighted structures; I recommend red and black wire. Be sure to leave plenty of slack so you can lift the structure or turn it on its side.

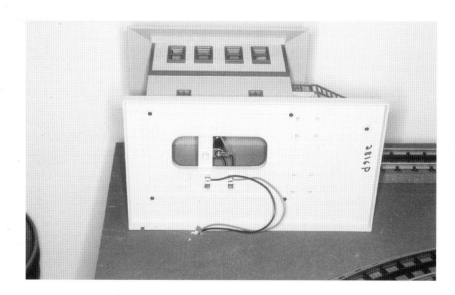

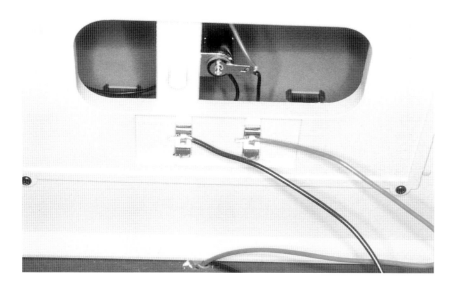

All of the ready-built structures have simple wire clips to hook into. Strip about ⅛ inch off the ends of the wire, twist it (if it's stranded), push the clip back, and insert the wire.

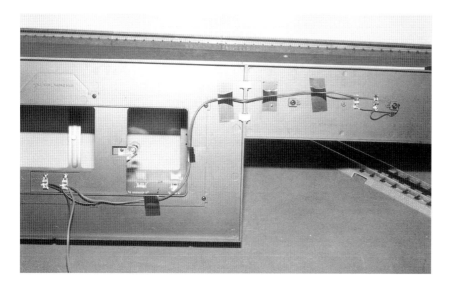

For large structures like MTH's beautiful railroad station, use strips of electrical tape to secure the wiring to the base of the structure.

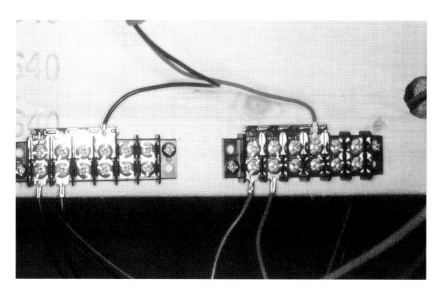

Position terminal strips in a location under the train board so you can minimize the lengths of wire bundles from the terminal strips to the structures. The upper two wires go back to the switch on the control panel. The terminal jumper distributes power to all the screws it is attached to, and the lower wires come from the individual structures.

An Atlas connector is nothing more than a set of three switches. The wires on the left side go to the power source, while each switch has two screw posts. The power coming in from the left side is distributed to all the switches so all we need to do is run the two wires from the top of the terminal strips under the train board to these two screw posts.

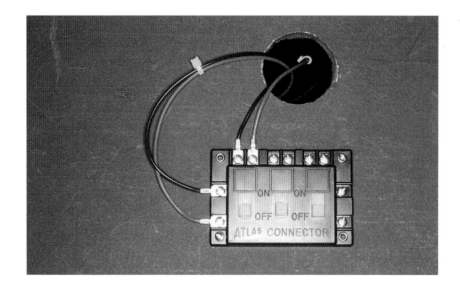

All the MTH ready-made structures are now wired and ready to be tested. Since an external power source is needed for the lights, I replaced the MTH Z-750 transformer with the MTH Z-4000 transformer, which can supply both 10 and 14 volts to run accessories.

Next, I positioned the yard lights along the track siding and then drilled individual holes for the wiring.

These die-cast metal lights are easy to hook up. I used telephone wire for these applications because it's inexpensive, and the wire is solid which means that you can shape it. Radio Shack sells lengths of this telephone wire, which has four colored wires: red, black, yellow, and green. In most applications I simply use two wires—red (hot) and black (ground).

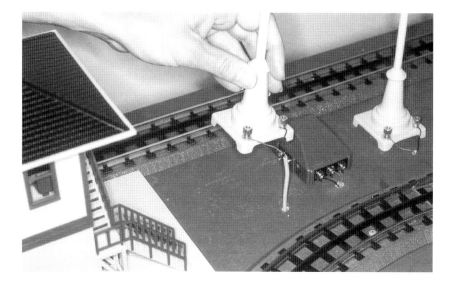

Be sure to leave some slack in the wiring so you can lift the light fixture up off the train board.

The die-cast yard lights have all been connected to the terminal strips, and power from the Atlas connector has also been attached. I used the second switch on the Atlas connector for the die-cast lights. Notice how the tie strips help keep wire bundles together as well as minimize the messy appearance of large quantities of wires. One last thing to do is flip the switch and test the lights.

The ready-made MTH structures and the first set of die-cast lamps have been installed and everything is wired. It's time to take a break, turn off the room lights, flip on the house and streetlights, and run some trains.

Parking Lot Lights

I positioned the parking lot lights for the train station and drilled holes in the plywood for the wiring. When drilling into the open areas of the plywood, be sure to position the accessories so as to avoid the underside framing. Otherwise you will be drilling through the plywood and a 2 x 4!

The screw posts on some of the die-cast lights have holes in them, which makes attaching the wires very easy. Also note that one terminal post is insulated from the rest of the accessory.

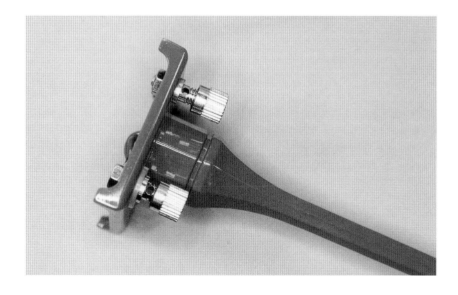

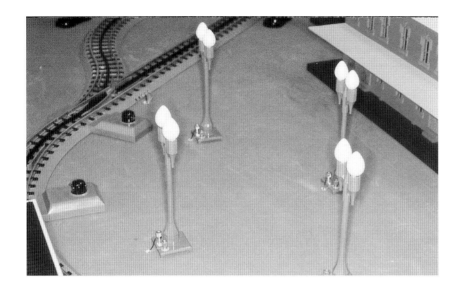

Now that the parking lot lamp posts are wired, it's time to attach the wires to the terminal strips.

Since I planned to have all the die-cast streetlights controlled by one of the Atlas connector switches, I added these wires to the yard light terminal strips.

Platform Lights

These station platform lights were the next to be installed. Some of the holes had to be drilled through the 2 x 4 framing because of the locations of the lights.

These die-cast station lights have wire clips in place of the screw posts. The clips can be stiff, so use a small screwdriver to loosen the wire clip.

Here the wires have been attached. Note that the insulation on the wire has been removed only far enough to attach to the clip.

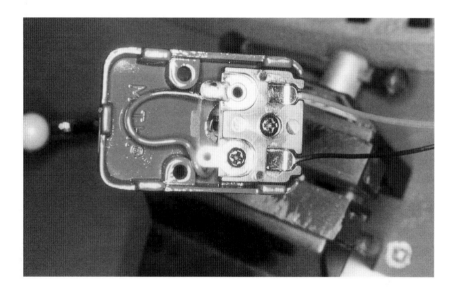

The station lights have now been installed, and it's time to test the entire setup.

With the addition of so many lights the layout is starting to take shape and look busy. The boys really like running the trains in the dark with all the layout lights on.

Streetlights

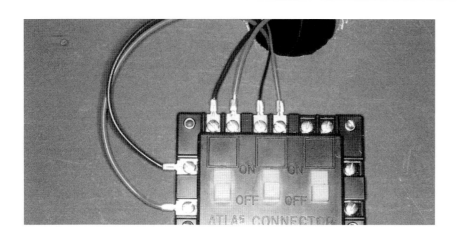

Because one more switch was left on the Atlas connector, I decided to add some small streetlights to the area where the houses are.

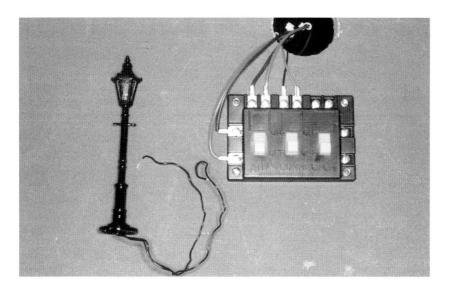

The wires attached to these small lamps are also stripped. I tested the lights by touching the wires to the screw posts on the left side of the Atlas connector.

I positioned the streetlights along the edges of where I planned to have the street and then drilled the holes for the wires.

Since the streetlight wires are very thin, I spliced them with special connectors available from Radio Shack. Just insert the wires (no need to strip them) into the connector and then use a pair of pliers to close the disk that splices through the wire and electrically connects them together.

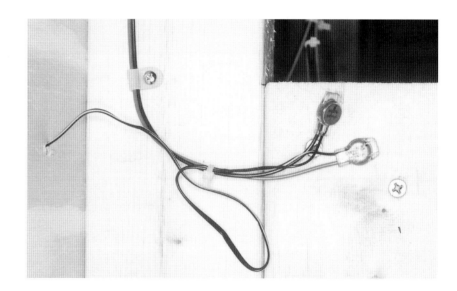

I ran out of terminal jumpers! No problem. I stripped a length of solid wire and then jumpered it to all the terminal strip screws. I connected the streetlights to the third Atlas connector switch, and then labeled all terminal strips to make it easier to troubleshoot any electrical problems.

The streetlights look like they don't belong, but once the street is painted they will look right at home.

Since I planned to also run a steam engine on this layout, I added a die-cast metal water column. No wiring necessary—hooray!

With the addition of accessories, the layout is starting to look busy and interesting.

Uncoupling Section

MTH supplies everything you need to hook up an uncoupler. If you want the controller to be located on the control panel, you'll have to make an additional bundle of wires just like you did for some of the switches. The first step is to add small strips of masking tape to the wires, label them, and then remove them from the uncoupler's screw posts.

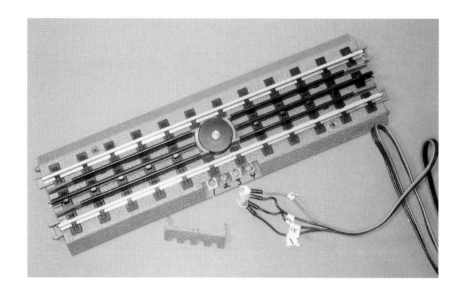

I positioned a terminal strip under the train board and then attached the labeled wires. Then I attached the telephone wire to the terminal strip and labeled each color (which I then wrote down) so that each label (1 through 4) had a corresponding colored wire.

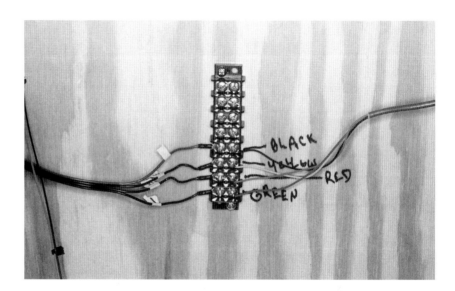

Next, I attached the colored wires to the corresponding screw post on the uncoupler.

Crossing Gates and Sensors

The crossing gate signals had quick-attachment wire clips that make wiring them quick and easy.

Next, I plugged in the infrared sensors at the far ends of the track so that the crossing gate signals would be activated by a train approaching from either direction. The crossing gate signal is a simple two-wire hookup to the common and "NO" screw terminals of the sensor.

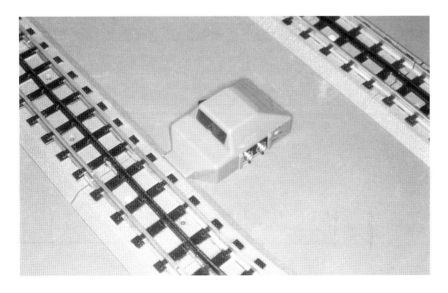

The two infrared beams emit from the red plate of the sensor, so it's important to protect the surface of this plate.

You can adjust the range of the sensor from as close as 1½ inches to as far away as about 14 inches.

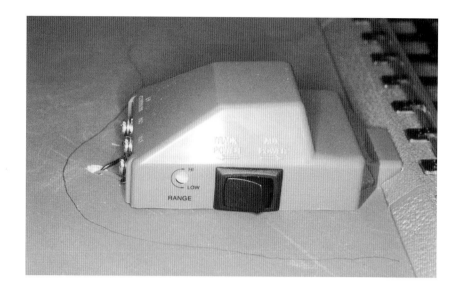

You can also adjust the delay time on the sensor. The delay time determines how long the accessory will remain activated.

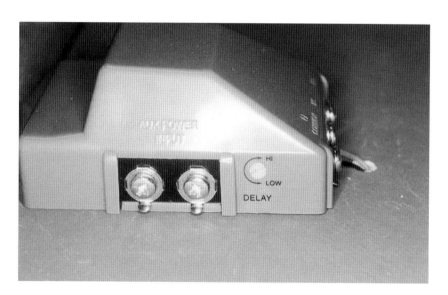

Both crossing gate signals have now been positioned and the wires that are dangling under the train board need to be hooked up.

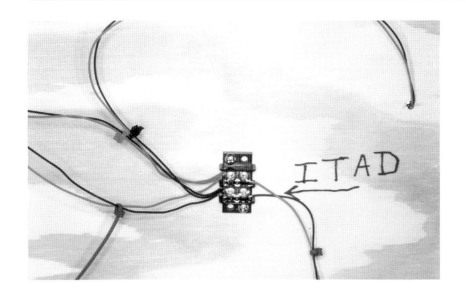

Since the infrared sensors draw their power from the track, there is no need to add an additional power source. You can even hook these sensors together so that you can activate an accessory from separate locations. Here two wires come from each sensor and from each crossing gate signal. To keep from mixing up the polarity of the sensors and the accessories, I used red and black wire.

This infrared sensor has a three-wire hookup to the block signal for the siding. Accessory hookups will use the common screw post and either or both of the "NC" and "NO" screw posts.

Now that all the accessories are installed and wired, it's time to run some trains to test the block signal and the crossing gate.

Control Panel and Testing

To help my boys runs the trains, I added labels to the Atlas connector switches. I also added some simple reminders on train operation.

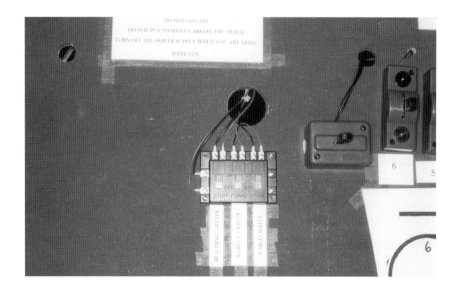

To help us with all the switch locations, I labeled the switch controllers and also added a simple layout diagram with the corresponding labels on the switches.

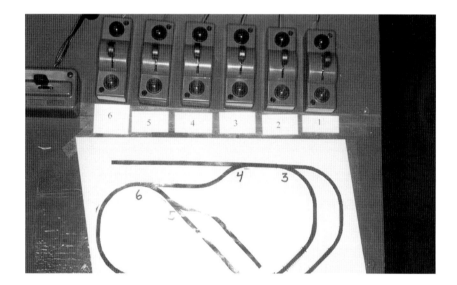

This is the eye-level view that a typical 6- to 10-year-old sees. This view looks pretty neat as the locomotive passes the switch tower.

Although this view is pretty mundane, once the scenery is added it will appear very different.

The infrared sensors worked well on the first test run, although it took a few minutes to get the range and delay adjustments set correctly.

Now that everything is working and the boys have gotten the knack of running the locomotive and throwing the switches, they couldn't be happier. Thomas is at the throttle while Gregory is "king of the switch controls."

Chapter Five

Adding Scenery to Your Layout

S o how do you turn your track-on-plywood toy train layout into something more realistic? It's simple. All it takes is some basic scenery supplies, some imagination, and some small helping hands—oh yes, and some "quality time."

Railroad layouts range from toy train, which is pretty much what we accomplished in Chapters 3 and 4, to hi-rail —"model-railroad-speak" for everything in scale except for the center rail. True hi-rail layouts are gorgeous, but they are the exception; the vast majority of us land somewhere between toy train and hi-rail. What is important is that you enjoy what you are doing and that you have created an atmosphere for you and your children to have fun and to exercise your imaginations.

everal companies sell scenery materials, and they are all pretty good. To simulate grass, dirt, and other types of ground coverings, you can buy bags or boxes of multi-colored materials. To simulate brush, plants, and bushes, you can buy different color foliage matting. You can buy ready-made trees of different sizes, shapes, and types, or you can buy tree kits and make your own. To vary the flat landscape of a train board, you can make elevations in the landscape by piling small amounts of fine sand and then covering it with the speckled colored covering. To make hills and mountains you can use newspaper, wire screening, tape, paper towels, and plaster, or plaster cloth. For coloring the mountains and painting streets, visit your local hardware store and have them mix various colors of brown for mountains, medium gray for streets, and dark green for the undercoating.

Streets

As a first step, use a black marker to outline where you want the streets, and then use lengths of masking tape to protect the track where streets cross them. For our layout, they're at the crossing gates. Next, mix the street paint. To simulate the rough appearance of paved streets, pour some medium gray paint into a small plastic bucket and start mixing small amounts of fine play sand into the paint. When the

mixture looks gravely, it's time to start painting. Use a small flat brush to run the paint along the black marker outlines, and then start painting the areas in between. Lift up the streetlights, the structures, and other accessories to paint under them. Now you know why I recommended that you have slack in the wiring of all your accessories! To keep the sand in suspension in the paint, you will need to stir the paint frequently.

Once you have covered the entire area, go back over it a second time, being sure to spread the sand-paint mixture evenly across the surface. Discard the remaining paint mixture, let the paint dry, and if necessary give it a second coat using a fresh sand-paint mixture.

Base coat

Once the gray street paint has dried, it's time to give the dark green train board a coat of earth color. You can use any brown ranging from tan to dark brown. The point is that when you add the ground cover you may miss some tiny spots. The brown undercoating color will help hide these. Besides, under any layer of grass there is brown dirt, and it shows through in places. Here again, to protect the track use masking tape to cover the sides. The taping will take you an hour or two, but it's well worth the effort, as children and paintbrushes do not equal neatness. Be sure to mask around any

street lamps that you may have screwed down, and also be sure to mask around the infrared sensors—especially red sensor faces!

Once you have completed the masking, paint the areas around the masking tape first to outline and box in the areas to be painted. Be careful when running the paintbrush next to the gray painted roads. Using the side of the brush with a moderate amount of paint will pretty much give you a nice even line between the gray road paint and the brown color.

Once you have boxed in the areas, paint the entire surface, let the paint dry, and then give it a second coat. After the paint has dried, remove the masking tape. The addition of two paint colors will make a dramatic change in the appearance of the train board.

Trees

Next let's add some trees. The tree trunks on ready-made trees are gray or brown plastic, but they are also shiny. To tone down the shine, apply a hobby paint clear dull coat. These clear dull coats can be either enamel-based or water-based. The water-based paints are safer.

Once the tree trunks and lower branches are painted with the dull coat, apply white glue to the bases of the trees and position them on the train board. Since trees grow just about anywhere, location is a matter of choice. Just don't get them too close to the right-of-way. My children painted the clear dull coat on the tree trunks and then positioned and glued the trees in place.

Ground cover

Now comes the really fun and messy part—spreading out the ground cover. You can find a variety of materials and products for this. I used a Woodland Scenics sifter, two bottles of their scenic cement, their scenic cement sprayer, and a small

flat paintbrush. Decide what color ground foam you want to spread out, and then pour some into the scenic sifter. Next pour some of the scenic cement into a cup and apply the cement to small areas at a time with your trusty paintbrush. I like to work in 1-foot squares or less because the cement dries quickly.

Using the sifter, spread out the ground cover. You will get the hang of this very quickly, and so will your children. The sifter will help you keep the ground cover concentrated in the area you painted with the cement.

Start out by applying the ground cover around the houses, being careful to have a good clean demarcation line between the ground cover and the gray street paint. Here again, lifting the accessories is a must, or the ground cover will get all over them. Using a dry paintbrush, remove excess ground cover from unwanted areas and from the tracks.

To seal the ground cover, spray the scenic cement with the sprayer. The ground cover color will appear dark because it's wet, but it will lighten up again once it dries. To protect the track, use a small length of cardboard to deflect the spray away from the track. Use a damp tissue to wipe away any excess ground cover that may have moved as a result of spraying. To keep things a little less messy, start from the inside areas and work towards the outside. As soon as you have finished with the sprayer, clean it with hot water to remove excess glue from the nozzle.

I used green-colored ground cover for the area around the houses and brown and dirt colors for the areas around the train station, the switch tower, and near the track. To provide some depth to the colors, I lightly sprinkled two shades of green over the brown. Then to offset the solid green grass color, I sprinkled on a lighter shade of green and some brown. Since trees usually have slightly elevated areas around the bases of their trunks, I simulated this by piling the ground cover at the bases of the trees. This also hid the round bases of the trees.

Hills

As I worked my way around the outer part of the track, I decided to add two small hills to the end that had the double oval track. A simple way to make elevations is to wad up newspapers and bunch them in the location where you want the hill. Secure the paper to the layout

board with masking tape. Next cut strips of plaster cloth (available at hobby shops), soak them for just about 10 seconds in a pan of warm water, and then lay them across the newspaper. Plaster cloth is very easy and fun to use, and in about 10 minutes you will have a hill. To cover up the small holes of the plaster cloth just work the plaster with your finger tips. The plaster will set in about 20 minutes or so.

Next, I mixed some plaster and applied it to the hills with a flat paintbrush to cover any remaining holes and to provide some shape to the surfaces of the hills. Once the second coat of plaster was dry, I painted the hills with medium tan paint and highlighted it with a slightly darker color.

I next sprinkled some earth-colored ground cover on the surfaces of the hills followed by some green. The ground cover settled on the horizontal surfaces and in the crevices of the hills. Then I sprayed some scenic cement to secure the ground cover. I also applied ground cover to the base of the hills to blend them into the surface of the train board.

As a last step, to simulate brush I cut strips of Woodland Scenics foliage, stretched out the foliage matting per the instructions, and then bunched up the matting. I then applied white glue to the underside of the foliage and positioned it in locations on the hills, at their bases, and in small amounts all over the train board.

As a last touch I visited local toy stores in search of 1/43 scale die-cast automobiles, which I positioned around the layout. While 1/43 scale is slightly larger than 1/48 (O) scale, the difference is unnoticeable, and these die-cast cars appear right at home on the layout.

So that's it; you're officially a model railroader—the toy train variety. But realize that this is only the beginning. Keep checking the hobby shop for new cars, locomotives, and accessories. Read books and magazines to learn about new products and modeling techniques that will improve your skills and results. Start doodling track plans—perhaps you can add on to this layout. I plan to! Attend hobby shows and swap meets. Join clubs and go to conventions. There's a whole world of model railroading fun out there.

Happy railroading to you and your children.

Woodland Scenics sells several different colors of easy-to-use material that simulates brush and scrub.

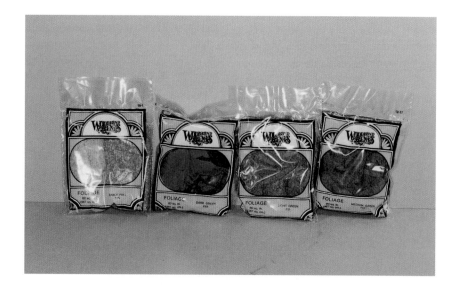

Life-Like Products sells ready-made trees of different shapes, sizes, and varieties. These trees look pretty realistic when added to the overall landscape of your layout.

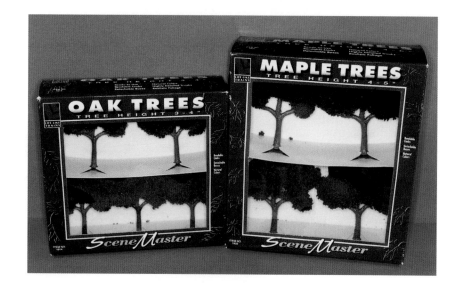

If you prefer to make your own trees, Woodland Scenics sells tree kits that are easy and fun to make.

For ground cover Life-Like products and Woodland Scenics sell ground cover material in various textures and colors.

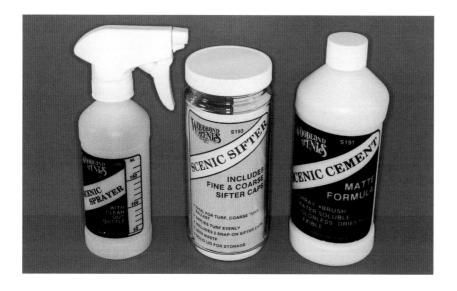

To properly lay ground cover you will need a sifter (center). You will also need a dilute glue (right) to attach the ground cover to the train board, as well as a sprayer (left) to seal the ground cover with the same glue. Woodland Scenics sells all three of these necessary products.

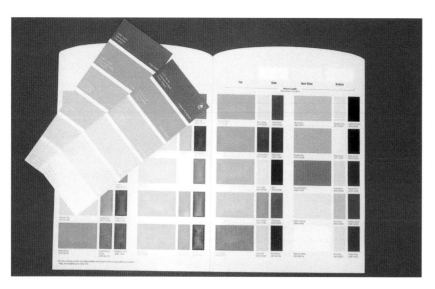

For painting hills and simulating paved streets, visit your local hardware or paint store and get some sample color sheets. They can mix any shade of water-based paint you want.

Quart-size cans provide all the paint you'll need for this or any other small layout. For the paved streets I selected a medium gray, and for the track layout undercoating and hills I chose a medium tan.

Streets and Parking Lots

The first step in adding scenery is to outline where you want to have your streets, parking lots, driveways, and walkways. I used a black marker with a medium point to draw these outlines.

Mixing the paint after the can is opened is important so the pigments of the paint are distributed properly for a consistent color.

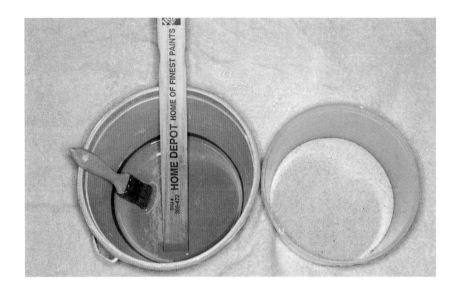

To simulate the rough surface of pavement, mix in some fine-grain play sand, available at most hardware stores.

Pour small quantities of sand into the paint bucket while you mix it.

You will know that you have enough sand in the paint when the paint looks grainy.

Before painting, protect the track by covering it with masking tape.

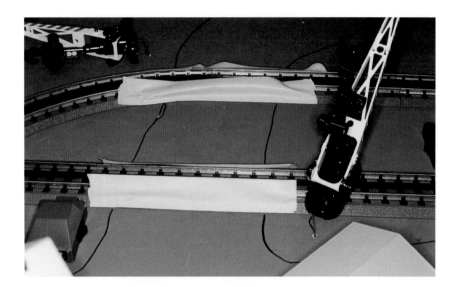

Using a flat brush, paint along the inner edge of the pavement outline.

To paint under accessories, simply lift them off the train board. This is why I recommended that you leave some slack in the wiring of the accessory.

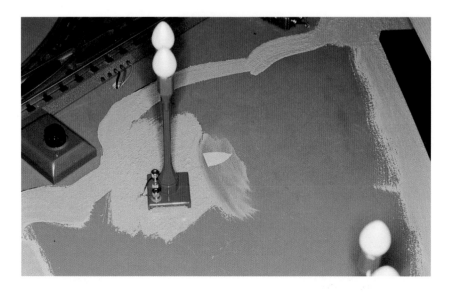

The train station parking lot has been outlined, and now it's time to paint between the lines. Be sure to mix the sand-paint mixture frequently, as the sand will constantly settle to the bottom of the bucket.

Before I painted between the lines on the station parking lot, I also painted the street and sidewalks where the houses are located.

Children love to paint, so I turned the paintbrush and bucket over to Thomas and let him finish the job.

To ensure that the sand-paint mixture is spread evenly across the surface, use a stippling motion (up and down) with the paintbrush if you apply a second coat.

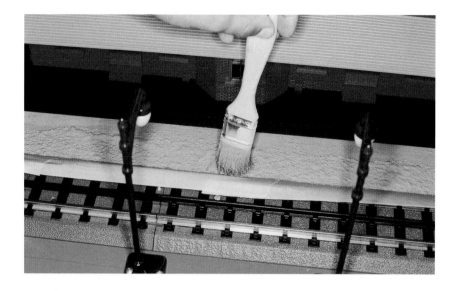

Masking

The train station parking lot and the street and sidewalks are done.

Now it's time to start masking the track around the train board so that you can apply the scenery undercoating.

The addition of the gray sand-paint mixture to the train board looks pretty strange at this point, but after we apply the tan paint undercoating to the rest of the surface, it will look a lot better.

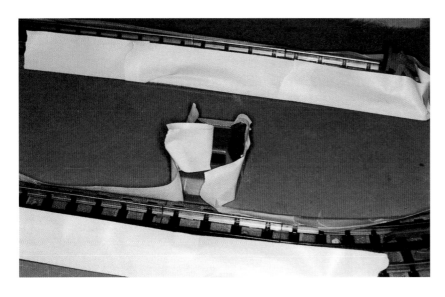

When masking the infrared sensors, be sure to cover the clear red sensor plate so there is no chance that paint will mar the surface.

These train station lights were screwed into the train board. It was easier to mask around them than to take out the screws.

To apply the tan color, use the outline technique and then let the children finish the job. To get a fine edge where the tan meets the gray or along the edges of the track, use the flat side of the brush.

Things are progressing nicely, and the boys did well. They even got more paint on the train board than they did on themselves!

The surface of the board is now completely covered, and the layout is starting to shape up. The gray paint doesn't seem to stand out as much as it did against the green.

Now that the masking tape has been removed, you can see the difference that the gray sand-paint mixture and the tan paint have made.

You can also see how the gray paint seeped under the masking tape at the gate crossing area! Either I applied too much paint, or the masking tape lifted off the track side.

The streets and sidewalks have good demarcation lines separating the colors, thanks to a small flat brush. Don't forget to paint in driveways for the cars!

The overall appearance of the train board has been improved greatly with the addition of these two paint colors. While you could add a few trees and some foliage and call it quits, a little extra work, some patience, and ground cover will dramatically change the appearance of the layout.

Trees

The first step in adding trees to the layout is to hide the shiny appearance of the plastic tree trunks and branches by giving them a coat of Testors Dullcote. While Dullcote is an enamel-based product, other manufacturers make comparable water-based products.

Apply Elmer's glue to the perimeter of the tree bases to attach them to the train board.

Don't worry about the glue squeezing out from under the tree bases. The ground cover will hide both the excess glue and the round bases. Give the glue about an hour to dry before starting to apply the ground cover.

Gregory liked positioning and gluing the trees in place around the surface of the train board. Since trees grow just about anywhere, picking locations is not critical.

Having said that, be sure to place trees around the houses, as it's rare to find a house without a least one tree nearby.

Now that all the trees have been glued to the layout, it's time to start applying the ground cover.

Ground Cover

I transferred the ground cover from the manufacturer's packages to resealable bags for easy storage. Working with ground cover can get kind of messy, so I recommend that *you* fill the sifters and let the kids do the sifting.

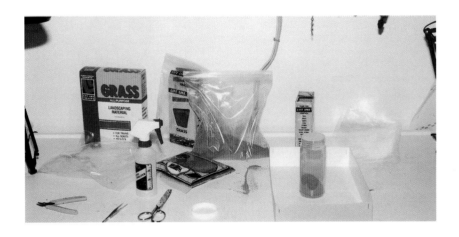

Use a brush to apply Woodland Scenics dilute glue mixture to small areas. Be sure to wipe off any excess that may get on the track, accessories, or sensors.

Next, sprinkle the ground cover onto the wet areas with your trusty sifter. You want to apply enough ground cover to hide most of the tan paint. After all, every lawn has brown patches here and there!

To seal the ground cover onto the surface, spray it with the Woodland Scenics dilute glue mixture. When you have finished using the sprayer, be sure to clean the nozzle with hot water to remove any excess glue. The glue will clog the nozzle unless it is cleaned thoroughly.

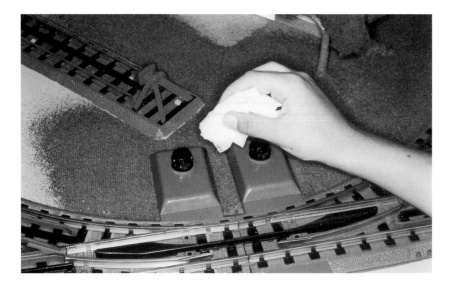

Use a damp tissue to wipe off excess glue and ground cover.

The ground cover and street edge does not have to be perfect. To help shape the edging, use a dry paintbrush to sweep away excess ground cover while it's still wet.

I used the greener ground cover around the houses and then sprinkled light dustings of brown in places where the simulated grass might logically be worn down.

To apply the ground cover, start in the center of the train board where it is harder to reach and work towards the outside.

Here brown ground cover has been added to outline the parking lot. Note how the tan undercoating blends into the ground cover.

Now that the inner areas of the layout are just about done, it's time to work our way around the outside. Use masking tape to protect accessories from getting coated with the ground cover.

Brown ground cover has been applied as the base color and then a light sprinkling of light green was added to break up the consistent brown color.

Since I had two shades of green, I sprinkled on a light dusting of the darker green color to offset the brown. Having a variation in color helps add realism to your layout, as you would seldom see dirt without at least a hint of something green growing in it.

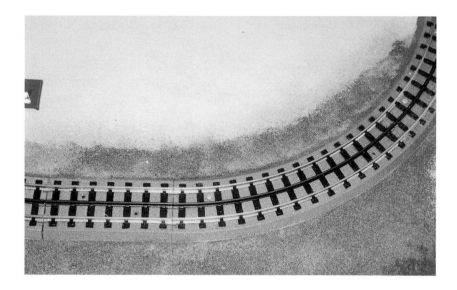

To cover the bases of trees, pile some ground cover next to them.

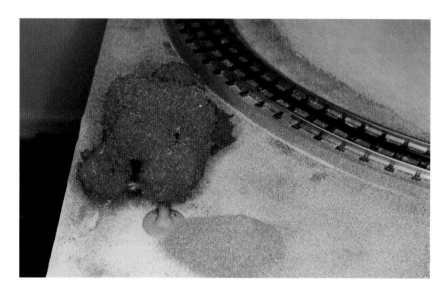

Carefully spread the ground cover around the base of the tree with a small brush and your finger. Note that I applied some fine-grain sand to a small area to simulate a sand pile.

The ground cover is slowly being worked around the outer areas of the layout. Note how the overall appearance is starting to change.

The ground cover has now been completely applied to almost the entire surface of the layout. Before we apply the ground cover to the remaining areas, let's add some hills.

Hills

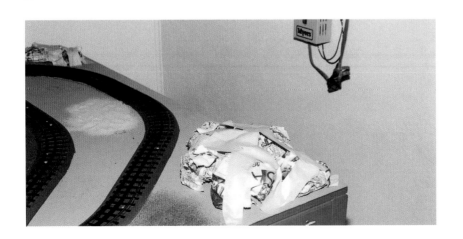

This pile of crumpled-up paper held in place with masking tape is all you need to form a small hill.

Next, cut strips of Woodland Scenics plaster cloth, dip them in a pan of warm water, and then lay them over the paper pile. To fill in the holes in the plaster cloth, simply run your fingers across the surface. Thomas was the plaster-cloth-hole-filler, as he always loves to get his hands messy.

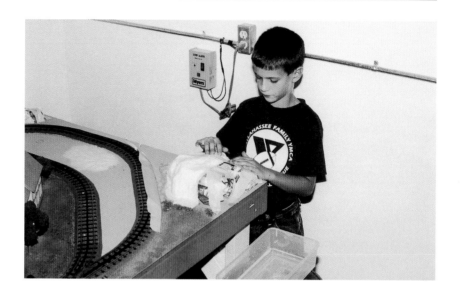

You have to set the plaster cloth in warm water for only about 5 to 8 seconds before it's ready to be applied. Gregory was our resident expert plaster-cloth-applicator specialist.

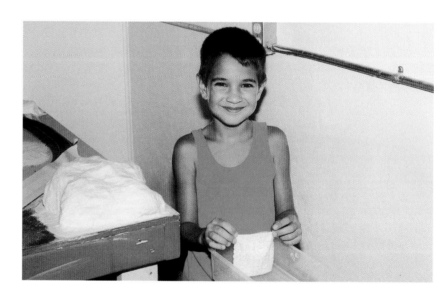

Here you can see that the first hill is just about finished. It doesn't look like much now, but just wait until we paint it!

Sometimes the shape of the plaster cloth looks a little odd, especially if there are some wrinkles. To help smooth out these areas, mix some plaster and use a flat brush to apply a coat over the plaster cloth.

Both hills are now complete and ready to be painted. Also note the sand pile. I liberally soaked it with Woodland Scenics white glue to hold it firmly in place. This small pile will add some height to an otherwise flat area.

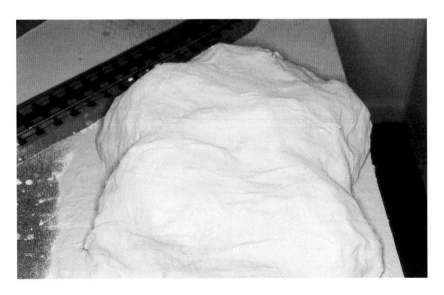

The hills have been painted with the same tan paint as the layout. Two coats were necessary to get into all the nooks and crannies.

The next step was to lightly dust brown and light green ground cover over the hills. The ground cover settled onto the horizontal surfaces, resulting in a very realistic effect. To seal the ground cover I sprayed it with Woodland Scenics glue.

Shrubs and Brush

The first step in using Woodland Scenics foliage is to cut a small piece and then stretch it out.

Once you have stretched it out, crumple it by folding the outer edges underneath its center. Now the foliage is ready to be added to the layout.

Small amounts of foliage look natural at the base of the hill and at the top.

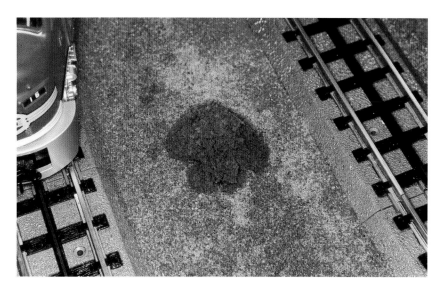

This small clump of foliage looks just like a bush or a shrub—using a little imagination, of course.

This foliage has been stretched out lengthwise to simulate a long clump of hedges. The foliage has been attached to the ground cover with some white glue applied to the underside of the foliage.

The overall appearance of the layout has now changed drastically with the addition of some basic scenery.

Now that the scenery is finally completed, it's time to run some trains!

Selected Books on Toy Trains

Listed below are a half-dozen or so books that pertain to building toy train layouts as well as a couple books intended for scale model railroading but which have toy train applications. All are published by Kalmbach Publishing Co. Kalmbach also publishes numerous guides and how-to books that pertain specifically to building layouts using Lionel trains. Check your local hobby shop for availability. You can also order these Kalmbach titles by phoning 1-800-533-6644, or you can order them online at http://www.kalmbachbooks.com

How to Build Model Railroad Benchwork, 2nd Ed.
How to Build Realistic Model Railroad Scenery, 2nd Ed.
Realistic Plastic Structures for Toy Trains
Realistic Railroading with Toy Trains
Realistic Track Plans for O Gauge Trains
Tips and Tricks for Toy Train Operators, 2nd Ed.
Track Plans for Toy Trains
Toy Train Collecting and Operating: An Introduction to the Hobby

Clubs, Organizations, and Magazines

American Flyer Collectors Club
P. O. Box 13269
Pittsburgh, PA 15243

Classic Toy Trains Magazine
Kalmbach Publishing Co.
21027 Crossroads Circle
P. O. Box 1612
Waukesha, WI 53187

Ives Train Society
P. O. Box 32017
Richmond, VA 23226

K-Line Collectors Club
P. O. Box 2831
Chapel Hill, NC 27515

Lionel Collectors Club of America
P. O. Box 479
La Salle, IL 61301

Lionel Operating Train Society
P. O. Box 62240
Cincinnati, OH 45241

Lionel Railroader Club
c/o Lionel Trains, Inc.
50625 Richard W. Blvd.
Chesterfield, MI 48051-2493

Marx Train Collectors Club
P. O. Box 111
Bakerstown, PA 15007

MTH Railroad Club
7020 Columbia Gateway Dr.
Columbia, MD 21046

National Association of S Gaugers
Paul Stevens
9619 NW 71 St.
Kansas City, MO 64152

National Model Railroad
    Association
4121 Cromwell Rd.
Chattanooga, TN 37421

Toy Train Collectors Society
Louis A. Bohn
109 Howedale Dr.
Rochester, NY 14616

Toy Train Operating Society
25 W. Walnut St., Suite 308
Pasadena, CA 91103

Train Collectors Association
P. O. Box 248
Strasburg, PA 17579

Manufacturers of Toy Trains and Toy Train–Related Products

(Most manufacturers do not sell directly to consumers. Always check your local hobby shop before contacting manufacturers.)

American Models
10087 Colonial Industrial Dr.
South Lyon, MI 48178
(S gauge locomotives and cars)

Arttista Accessories
105 Woodring Ln.
Newark, DE 19702
(Metal, hand-painted O scale figures and accessories)]

Atlas O
603 Sweetland Ave.
Hillside, NJ 07205
(O gauge cars, locomotives, track, and structures)

Bachmann Industries Inc.
1400 E. Erie Ave.
Philadelphia, PA 19124
(Snap-together building kits)

Bowser Manufacturing Co.
P. O. Box 322
Montoursville, PA 17754
(Three-rail trolleys, O gauge figures and detail parts)

CTT, Inc.
109 Medallion Center
Dallas, TX 75214
(Track planning templates for three-rail track)

Curtis Hi-Rail Products, Inc.
P. O. Box 385
North Stonington, CT 06359
(Three-rail switches and track products)

Dallee Electronics Inc.
246 W. Main
Leola, PA 17540
(Electronic devices and control systems)

GarGraves Trackage Corp.
8967 Ridge Rd.
North Rose, NY 14516
(Flexible three-rail and sectional track with wood ties)

K-Line
MDK, Inc.
P. O. Box 2831
Chapel Hill, NC 27515
(Three-rail O gauge trains and accessories)

Lionel LLC
50625 Richard W. Blvd.
Chesterfield, MI 48051-2493
(Three-rail electric trains, track, and accessories)

Marx Trains
367 W. Irving Park Rd., No. 338
Wood Dale, IL 60191-1325
(Metal, lithographed O gauge cars and locomotives)

Model Rectifier Corp.
80 Newfield Ave.
Edison, NJ 08837
(Control systems)

M.T.H. Electric Trains
7020 Columbia Gateway Dr.
Columbia, MD 21046
(Standard and O gauge locomotives, cars, track, and accessories)

QSIndustries
3800 S.W. Cedar Hills Blvd., No. 224
Beaverton, OR 97005
(Electronic reversing units and sound units)

Ross Custom Switches
45 Church St.
Norwich, CT 06360
(Three-rail switches)

S-Helper Service Inc.
77 Cliffwood Ave.
Cliffwood, NJ 07721
(S gauge cars and locomotives)

Third Rail
Sunset Models Inc.
37 S. Fourth St.
Campbell, CA 95008
(O scale locomotives)

United Model Distributors
301 Holbrooke Dr.
Wheeling, IL 60090
(O gauge cars)

Weaver Quality Craft Models
P. O. Box 231, RR 1
Northumberland, PA 17857
(Three-rail locomotives and rolling stock)

Williams Electric Trains
8835-F Columbia 100 Pkwy.
Columbia, MD 21045
(Three-rail locomotives and rolling stock)

Woodland Scenics
P. O. Box 98
Linn Creek, MO 65052
(Ballast and landscaping materials for all scales)

Index